Six Years at the Russian Court

Margaret Eager

Table of Contents

Preface

IN a book recently published the author describes at length a visit to the house of the Governor of Moscow, and speaks of his family and governess. Now for fourteen years before his death the Grand Duke Serge was Governor of Moscow and he had no children.

A well-known magazine spoke of us travelling with a cow! Now I can safely aver that I never took a cow on a journey. She would have been very much in our way, and the poor beast would have had a sad time in the Baltic or Black Sea! Again and again have I seen allusions to the Empress's love of caricatures, and her cleverness in drawing them. As a matter of fact, the Empress never drew such a thing in her life; nor can she see the fun of them when they are drawn by other people.

The author of a book which had considerable success describes Tsarskoe Selo as being surrounded by double walls of granite. As a matter of fact, Tsarskoe Selo is separated from the road only by iron railings. The English daily papers described the Emperor and his family as having fled in their yacht, at a time when the yacht was deeply embedded in ice outside Kronstadt.

I could multiply such stories ad lib., but merely wish to draw attention to the fact that so much that is written regarding Russia and the Imperial family is absolutely untrue, so little is really known about the Court life, that I am emboldened to offer my slight sketches of life in the Palaces. It would be very easy for me to "pile on the agony;" to represent the Emperor as a "much ridden" man; to picture plots and counter plots; to speak of hairbreadth escapes from death; of hidden bombs; of life made horrible by fears; but no such things have occurred in my six years at the Russian Court, and I am a truthful person, and have not started forth to write fiction, but plain, unvarnished truth. To the courtesy of the editor of the Leisure Hour I am indebted for permission to reprint those parts of this work which have already appeared in print. But the book has been considerably enlarged.

M. Eagar.

London, 1906.

5

NOTE.

SHORTLY after the birth of the Czarovitch I said to the Empress that I often had thought of writing my memoirs. She encouraged me to do so, saying so many untruths had been published that it would be a relief to have an account of the Russian Court which was absolutely true. Hence this book.

Chapter I: Concerning my Journey

IT was late in 1898 that I was chosen to take charge of the little Grand Duchesses of Russia, and early the following year I set off for the land of the Czar.

It had been arranged that a Royal messenger should meet me in Berlin, and I was to have travelled under his escort to St. Petersburg. But in case of any failure of the plan, the friend who had kindly undertaken to smooth all difficulties in the travelling gave me a telegram for the Empress's Chancellor to be sent off from the frontier.

On arriving in Berlin I was met by a servant from the Embassy, armed with an immense white linen bag, tied round with red tape and sealed with several great seals. To my dismay I was asked to take charge of the bag and deliver it safely to a messenger from the Embassy in St. Petersburg, who should meet me at the station there.

The ambassador sent me a letter telling me that I should in no wise lose sight of the bag on the journey, and that I should not allow it to be examined by the Custom House officials, nor by the Police.

Before leaving England I had been told that the Empress would send a servant to the frontier to meet me, who would look after my luggage and help me generally on the rest of the journey; so, feeling sure that my troubles would end there, I undertook the charge of the bag. I fear that had I known the trouble it would be to me before the end of the journey, I should have declined to be burdened with it.

I had been given a passport for the bag, and on arriving at the frontier, I walked up to a gentleman in uniform, presented the passport, and asked if there was anyone to meet me. There was no one, but the gentleman gave me into the charge of a porter and told him to help me, so I followed him about like a pet dog, only refusing to part with my precious bag.

I sent off a telegram to the Winter Palace, and had my luggage examined. Oh! What an examination it was! Everything I possessed was turned out of my trunks, and they even put their hands into my boots and gloves. I then had to pay sixpence for the examination of each trunk.

Finally, I heard my name called by an official, so made my way to him and received my passport, which had been taken up for examination. All being in order, I was at last released from durance vile; so I took my precious bag in my arms, and seated myself in the train. I had lunched at the frontier, as in Russia the trains have no dining-cars; travellers have difficulty in securing refreshment on the way. The bag weighed heavily on my mind, and I dared not leave it unprotected in the train. I could not carry it in my arms to the refreshment-rooms, so I made up my mind that I should have to go without food.

Fortunately a lady in the train took compassion upon me, and with the help of a friend procured me a cup of tea and a sandwich. I may say here that the Russians are sympathetic and kind to a degree, and they are always willing to help a stranger in any way in their power.

My kind friend soon left. I then met with a rather unpleasant experience. The guard, on looking at my ticket, compelled me to change my carriage, as I had been travelling second-class with a first-class ticket. The compartment was very warm and the night very cold, so the difference of temperature was very trying, and I felt nervous and frightened. In solitary grandeur I continued my journey to St. Petersburg, where my precious bag and I safely arrived. I was met by a lady from the Winter Palace.

In vain I looked for someone to relieve me of the bag. On arriving at the Winter Palace, according to the Empress's orders I had lunched and retired. I had not long been asleep when I was roused by knocking at the door, and I, believing it to be Madame G., called out, "Come in." To my surprise a young man entered the room, saying, "I've come for that bag."

I begged him to leave the room until I rose and dressed. I felt doubtful at first about giving him the bag, but finally did so. His reason for coming to my room himself for it was that a servant in the Palace told him, when inquiring for me, that an English lunatic had arrived, carrying a great bag which she would not give up to anyone, so his only chance of getting it was to come up for it himself !

Hardly was he gone when Madame G. returned to conduct me to the Empress. I thought her then, and think her now, the handsomest woman I had ever seen. She is tall, statuesque in appearance, with very regular features and a high complexion.

She was wearing a mauve dress, as the mourning for the Queen of Denmark was not over. It was also the 2nd of February, the Purification of the Virgin, and a great feast in Russia, and Russians never wear black during a festival. The Empress received me in her boudoir -a lovely room, upholstered in mauve and silver brocade; the walls were hung with the same fabric, with a frieze of white wood decorated with trails and wreaths of wisteria painted on the wood. Wreaths of the same graceful plant adorned the ceiling. The furniture was made of Russian white wood.

She herself conducted me to the nurseries, where I saw my future charges, who were beautifully dressed, in honour of the festival, in transparent white muslin dresses trimmed with Brussels lace, and worn over pale-blue satin slips. Pale-blue sashes and shoulder ribbons completed their costumes. The little Grand Duchess Olga was at this time over three years of age. She was a very fine child, and had large blue-grey eyes and long golden curls. The Grand Duchess Tatiana was a year and a half; a very pretty child, remarkably like her mother, but delicate in appearance.

The Winter Palace is the largest building in Europe. It was begun by Peter the Great and finished by Catherine II., and is built in red sandstone. On one side there is a little enclosed garden, where in fine weather the children played and snowballed one another. The snow in the north of Russia does not cling together; it is too dry and powdery.

This garden is now enclosed by a red stone wall, surmounted by beautifully wrought iron railings, which were exhibited at the Paris Exhibition. I never saw the garden free from snow, but have been told that in summer it is beautiful with roses and lilac.

Chapter II: Concerning the Winter

A DESCRIPTION of this beautiful Winter Palace may prove interesting. I have mentioned that it is the largest building in Europe; it also contains the finest staterooms. Besides these state-rooms it has fifteen hundred other rooms. The Imperial nurseries are very large, and when I explain that one of the rooms is large enough to hold a "mountain" down which the children toboggan, some idea will be given of its magnitude. This room is upholstered in red, and here the royal children are taught dancing, and are sometimes joined in their lessons by cousins or friends. The little grand duchesses already dance well and gracefully.

From this room is entered the yellow room. Here walls and furniture are covered with a yellow brocade, and here are kept the children's various toys. From this room the principal living-room is entered, which overlooks the quay and Neva, also the garden. It is very sunny and bright, and is furnished in blue. A plain velvet pile blue carpet covers the floor. The walls are covered with cornflower patterned chintz. Very sweet and charming it is. From this two bedrooms are entered. Both are upholstered with pink and green chintz, and have plain velvet pile carpets in green. In one of them hangs a copy of Josephine Swaboda's beautiful Madonna and Child.

Over the children's rooms are those of the Empress. I have spoken of her boudoir. On one side of it is the Emperor's study, the most used room in the Palace. Here the Emperor spends hours each day working hard for the advancement of the great Empire committed to his charge. This room is plainly and solidly furnished. It overlooks the garden.

On the other side of the boudoir is the Empress's bedroom. It is also furnished in cloth from ceiling to floor. On this are displayed the holy images, and here hangs the sacred lamp which is always kept burning before the icons. Many of these pictures are illuminated in gold, and ornamented with precious stones. Some have the face simply painted and the garments all composed of precious stones. They are beautiful specimens of the goldsmiths' work, but are hardly artistic.

In this room are kept the Empress's jewels in glass cases. Many of her jewels are unique. On one occasion the Emperor gave her an ornament in the shape of a spray of tea-roses all executed in yellow diamonds. The spray consists of a full-blown rose, with four or five buds and leaves, all life-size. Her rubies and emeralds are very fine, and, of course, her diamonds are famous. The Grand Duchess Serge, sister to the Empress, is possessed of what are considered the finest sapphires in the world. Very splendid they are, both in colour and size, but the Empress has some which run them very closely.

From the bedroom we enter the yellow room. This room is crowded with lovely and artistic objects, and here are exhibited the famous Easter eggs which were at the Paris Exhibition. These are the work of Fabergé, the most renowned goldsmith in Europe. Beyond this are two other reception-rooms looking on to the quay and Neva, and then comes the dining-room, with its treasures of Bohemian and cut engraved glass. Beyond the dining-room is the Malachite room, about forty feet long. The walls have beautifully painted panels, divided by Malachite pillars; the furniture is Malachite and gilt, upholstered in crimson brocade, the floor parquet and polished like a mirror. These rooms are never shown to the public.

Then come the state rooms - great lofty halls lighted by electricity. The great white ballroom holds five thousand guests easily, allowing a place for the musicians and also space for dancing; but of course at these great functions there is little dancing.

The walls of these halls are covered with gold plates and dishes, many of them with the monograms of dead and gone Emperors and the double-headed Eagle in precious stones. Upon these dishes were presented formerly the bread and salt with which members of the Imperial family are greeted on entering a town. When an Imperial train stops at a station, a deputation of the principal persons, headed by one called the Stavosta or Elder, presents the Emperor with bread and salt. Shortly after the accession of Nicholas II., he found that the poorer villages and communities were unable to afford the expense of the gold plate, and yet could not bear to be outdone by the richer villages. He therefore issued a decree that henceforth bread and salt should be presented only on wooden or china dishes. This is very characteristic of his thought for his poorer subjects.

But to return to the Winter Palace. Another room has eight pairs of doors of tortoiseshell embellished with gold. At the end of all these great rooms is the theatre. My little charges would sit for half an hour at a time seriously looking while the attendants changed the drop scenes, and turned on the various coloured electric lights for their entertainment. This they called "going to the theatre." Beyond the theatre are the suites assigned to the various ministers and officers and their families. Returning from the theatre, but going round the other side of the Palace, we come to the Hermitage, with all its art treasures. In the picture gallery here is the finest collection of Rembrandts extant. One of these represents the visit of the Trinity to Abraham. I was one day looking at it, trying to make out what it meant, when the little Grand Duchess Olga ran up to me, and, putting her hand in mine, asked me what I was looking at. I told her; she then looked at it earnestly, and suddenly burst out laughing, exclaimed: "Oh! What a very funny picture - a man holding a leg of mutton in his hand, and carving it with a knife, and a bird sitting at the table." The bird, needless to say, was one of the angels. He is represented with his back out, and has neatly folded his blue-and-white feather wings. There are very many beautiful pictures, but I always thought the arrangement bad. They are arranged according to schools, Dutch school, etc., all together. So one gets sacred subjects mixed up with many very different pictures.

There is a great collection of Rubens' pictures, but I cannot say that I admire them much.

In the museum are many relics of Peter the Great. His turning lathe, a great deal of his carving, presses, chests, etc.; also the horse he used to ride stuffed in company with his dogs. There is a long staff showing his height. He must have been about six feet six inches. Therefore, in many respects he deserved the title of "Great," but he was exceedingly cruel. There is a goblet so constructed as to appear much less than it really is. Whenever he wished to "remove" any person he sent for him, flattered him with many kind words, and then, filling this goblet with strong wine, commanded the obnoxious person to drink it off to his health. When he had finished the contents of the goblet the victim fell dead upon the floor.

The museum also contains a splendid collection of jewelled snuff-boxes, presented to former Emperors by monarchs, ambassadors, and other great personages, jewelled watches, swords, harness, uniforms, etc.

There are also some very extraordinary portraits in mosaic work, mechanical animals and birds in silver and gold. The little children loved to ramble through this museum. When the Grand Duchess Olga was quite a little child she used to wish she could live there altogether. Here and there amongst the state-rooms are pretty winter gardens. In one of them is an aviary with hundreds of canaries, which are allowed to flit amongst the palms. There are also fountains with goldfish. Catherine II loved musical surprises in various forms, and there are writing-tables and presses, which, on being opened, play various tunes. These were a great joy to my little charges.

Chapter III: Concerning St. Petersburg

ST. PETERSBURG itself is both interesting and beautiful. Essentially modern - it is only about two hundred years since it was built - it somehow conveys the impression of antiquity, and this in spite of the fact that the streets are wide and handsome, there are great open spaces, town gardens and boulevards. The idea of a town of the Middle Ages may be conveyed by means of the signboards; for each shop hangs out pictures illustrative of what may be found within. Thus a military tailor has pictures of uniforms, a greengrocer displays paintings of cauliflowers, etc. Vegetables, by the way, are exceedingly dear in the winter in St. Petersburg; cabbages are grown in hot houses. The peasants, however, use salted cabbage for their beloved soup.

The Russians tell you that the signboards are for the benefit of foreigners who cannot read Russian. It may be so; in this case St. Petersburg owes much of her picturesqueness to the stranger within her gates. She owes more than that, however, to strangers, for most of her commerce is in the hands of foreigners. The Russians themselves seem to have little aptitude or care for business. I sometimes think that St. Petersburg owes more of her beauty to the climate, and peculiar costumes than to her signboards. The air is very clear, and for the greater part of the winter clear blue skies prevail, and there is a great deal of sunshine. Cold sunshine it is, but even so, it is better than the fogs of London.

The Russian coachman wears a great fur-lined robe, reaching to his feet and belted in with a bright galon, a flat velvet cap, in blue, yellow, or red, according to the rank of his employer, finishes his costume. The sledge itself is picturesque. Usually drawn by a pair, or three horses, almost covered with a fine network of blue or red lined with silk to keep the frozen snow from being dashed back into the occupant's face. Skimming along over the frozen snow, it is indeed a pretty object.

Then the Russian priests, with their soutanes, low-brimmed hats, and long flowing hair, though not always so clean as fastidious mortals might wish, are distinctly picturesque, as also are the peasant women, clad in national costume, bright red, blue, mauve or yellow sarafans, with paletots to match, trimmed with silver or gold braid, and wearing the Kokoshnik, or crescent-shaped head-dress. St. Petersburg is, however, the most unsanitary town in Europe. The drainage is defective, and the habits of life are not healthy. A prince will live on the ground or first floor of his mansion, and the rest of the house will be let out. In the cellars poor families are crowded together; sometimes as many as twenty people live in one room. If any epidemic breaks out among them they say "It is the will of God." Small-pox is rife, and there is generally a good deal of typhoid fever. The water of the Neva is absolutely poisonous, and yet from the Neva St. Petersburg depends for the most part for her water supply. A good trade is done by selling drinking water from the Duderhoff hills, or from Tsarskoe Selo, which is situated about twenty miles from the capital, and where there is good spring water. I must say Peter the Great chose the site for his city with very little regard for the health of the residents.

Chapter IV: Concerning St. Petersburg

A FEW weeks after my arrival in Russia we went to Tsarskoe Selo - the name means "The Tsar's Borough." It is a pretty little town, surrounded by great forests, and has a population of a couple of thousand souls. The forests are for the most part evergreen, though there are also silver birch, oak, and ash trees. There are two palaces in this little town. The Great, or Catherine's Palace, and the Little, or Alexander's Palace, which she built for her grandson, Alexander I. We resided in the latter. It is a white Grecian building with a green roof. It is situated in a pretty park, and stands quite close to the road. It has two wings and the main body. In one wing live the Emperor, Empress, and the children, with their households. When I first went to Russia the children's suite was small, though pretty, but now the nurseries at Tsarskoe Selo are very fine, consisting of about eleven rooms. In the bathroom is a stationary bath of solid silver, used for the bigger children. There is a small silver bath for the use of whatever baby reigns. Each child's name is engraved upon it, so it forms a historical record. It was apparently bought for Nicholas I., and bears his name and those of his family. We also find the names of Alexander II., and of Marie, afterwards Duchess of Edinburgh. The last name added was that of Alexis, the little baby who was born in August, 1904.

The walls of all the new rooms are painted in oil with beautifully executed friezes of the same flowers as appear in the chintz, interspaced with golden butterflies or birds. The bathroom has sea-gulls painted on the frieze. At the end of this suite is the play room. It has eight windows overlooking the park and gardens. It is all yellow and green, like a bunch of daffodils, and has a frieze of peacocks strutting about amidst greenery. The carpet is a pale sage green, unpatterned. Over each window is a panel, in painted poker work, each representing some scene in animal or bird life. There are two fireplaces in this great room, but as the rooms are all heated with hot air, the fires are not required excepting for ventilation.

Catherine II. must have loved lilac, for the parks at Tsarskoe Selo are full of it. There are as many as eight different varieties, and in the summer evenings the perfume is delicious. I have been told that she sent into all countries and paid fabulous prices for some of the specimens. However, they have repaid the trouble she took. In some places the bushes look like great bouquets, so full and round are they, and there are several avenues lined on each side with it.

The park is fourteen miles in circumference. Catherine had very good ideas about laying out a park or gardens, also the building of a palace. There are great halls and state-rooms lined with marble. There is a great deal of pale-blue marble which is so exceedingly rare; also pink and yellow marble. The person who "Dreamt that she dwelt in marble halls" might awaken there and find her dream realised.

The great palace contains the far famed Amber-room. All the walls are inlaid with mosaic work of amber in different shades. Chairs, tables, and ornaments are carved in it. This room was prepared by her father for one of the former Empresses of Russia. President Loubet had a suite of rooms in this palace. There are many fine pictures. There is a great banqueting hall with twenty-eight windows in it, and here is the church which the Imperial family attend.

Between the two parks are the Little Caprice and the Great Caprice. The story goes that on one occasion Catherine II, walking with a favourite and trusted Minister in the park, complained of the flatness of the country, saying that it would give her great pleasure to come out the following morning and find a hill just where she stood. To hear was to obey. The minister started work immediately. The entire population of the country side was impressed. The work was carried on throughout the night, an arched way of stone was raised across the road, by excavating and digging, and a hill actually appeared before morning. This hill was afterwards covered with trees and shrubs.

Catherine II was an autocrat. She had a great objection to members of her household getting married. On one occasion a lady and gentleman belonging to her suite became engaged. For a long time Catherine refused her consent to their marriage, but finally agreed on the express condition that she was allowed to make all arrangements for the wedding. To this proposition they gladly consented. The ceremony concluded, she led the way down to the frozen Neva, where she had caused an ice house to be built. In this terrible abode she incarcerated them. Months after, when the Neva was in flood, their dead bodies were recovered and buried.

The Great Caprice is crowned by a Chinese pagoda, and in the park are Chinese bridges, a model of a Chinese village, and a theatre in the Chinese style. Even in Catherine's reign the Far East seemed to have attractions for the Russian mind. It is more than a hundred years since she died, and the cost of producing and bringing all these things from China must have been enormous. In Gatchina, the Dowager Empress's place in the Duderhoff hills, there is a Chinese gallery, all the contents of which were collected by Paul I, Catherine's most unhappy son.

Paul was a curious mixture. Some of his laws only came into force within the past ten years, and are wise and good. He ordained that only the children and grandchildren of Emperors should bear the title of Grand Duke, and have an allowance from the country. After that they should be known as Prince and Princess, with the Christian name; they should then have no allowance from the country and should be free to marry amongst the nobility. On the other hand, he had so exalted an opinion of his own importance that he commanded that when his carriage or sleigh passed all other carriages they should be brought to a standstill and the occupants should kneel on the road, without regard to age, sex, or infirmity.

Koskiusko, the Polish rebel, lived in his reign. He was arrested and imprisoned, and we find Paul liberating him on his promise never again to take up arms against him. Koskiusko loyally kept his word and refused to join in any plot for the liberation of his country.

A man of such an extraordinary character as Paul could hardly have been an unmixed blessing in the domestic circle. He was twice married and had a large family. Two of his sons, Alexander and Constantine, formed a resolution to force him to resign. With this object in view the sons entered the palace one night, each at the head of his regiment. They stationed themselves in the rooms at either side of Paul's bedroom, and sent in a deputation to try to prevail upon him to resign the crown in favour of his eldest son Alexander. It is probable that he could not see the rights of his eldest son so clearly as Alexander did, so the deputation, being unsuccessful, found a pillow a handy argument, and smothered him. When they left the room they gave orders that Alexander was forthwith to be proclaimed Emperor as the old Emperor was dead.

Alexander I had no children. His end is uncertain; he died suddenly on a voyage. For some unknown reason there was no lying in state, nor was the body embalmed, so the peasants throughout Russia believed that he did not die but went on a pilgrimage to Siberia, that his life has been miraculously lengthened out, and at some time when Russia has need of him he will come forth and vanquish his enemies, as he defeated Napoleon Bonaparte. There is reason to believe that he committed suicide and his face was too much disfigured to be seen.

He was succeeded by his younger brother Nicholas, against whom England fought in the Crimean War. Constantine should have succeeded Alexander, but he had fallen in love with and married a Polish countess, therefore renounced his claim to the throne.

Peter the Great, and all his successors with one exception, lie in the Fortress Church of St. Peter and St. Paul in St. Petersburg. This church is kept in most beautiful order. Fresh flowers are always there, and the holy lamps are kept burning continually on the tombs. The church itself is very pretty and contains many specimens of Peter the Great's work. Indeed, we find so much work attributed to him that the question arises, "How did he find time for so much handicraft?"

Chapter V: Concerning Easter

THAT year spring came unusually early and when we returned to St. Petersburg for Easter the river was already open for navigation, so we did not see the ceremony.

Easter is the great feast of the year in Holy Russia. The long severe fast of seven weeks is over. Many people in Russia eat no meat, butter, eggs, or milk, all through Lent. In the palace, however, we only observed three weeks - the first, fourth, and last. Many of the suite also fasted every Wednesday and Friday. The week before Lent begins is called" Butter week."

Russian pancakes are served twice a day. The Russians begin their lunch or dinner with pancakes, and they are eaten with caviar and sour cream. During the sixth week the great fair called Verba is held. The word means willow, and the fair is so called because great bunches of willow wands covered with catkins are sold. These wands are carried into the churches on Palm Sunday and are blessed by the priests; they are then carried home and carefully placed in jars of water in the windows of the houses. They soon begin to bud and throw out roots. They are allowed to remain until Whitsuntide, when they are taken into the country and planted. These wands are supposed to be typical of the palms spread before our Saviour.

At the Verba one finds many pretty and curious things. Russian lace and needlework may be picked up at very moderate prices; there are also quaint Russian toys and all manner of wooden articles. They also sell little figures in small bottles; these figures jump up and down in the funniest fashion when the piece of skin on the top of the bottles is pressed down. They are called American devils, but last year the name was changed to Japanese devils. There are also thousands of the coloured eggs which are indispensable to a Russian Easter. We used to colour a couple of hundred every Good Friday, in the nurseries. It was a great pleasure to the children, but rather dirty work. However, Easter, like Christmas, comes but once a year.

On Thursday in Passion Week the children went to Holy Communion. This yearly Communion is always a great festival and holiday in Russia, for the Russian church administers the Sacrament is only once a year. In preparation for it the candidate fasts for a week, going to church both morning and evening for the seven days. He then confesses his sins to the priest, receives absolution and asks pardon of all in the house who might have been offended during the past year. On the morning of the day a special costume is donned, married women generally keep their wedding dress for those occasions; they also wear a cap, while the unmarried women go bare-headed to the Sacrament.

The bread is broken into the wine and water and is administered with a spoon, a napkin having been tied round the neck of the communicant. On returning from the church all the friends come forward and present their congratulations, flowers and bonbons are sometimes given, and the rest of the day is observed as a holiday. The rite of Confirmation is administered immediately after baptism, and children up to the age of seven years can receive the Communion as often as every month. After that age confession and church-going are essential, before receiving the Communion.

The little Grand Duchess Olga made her first confession in Moscow, during Lent, 1903, and she received a gift from the children of Moscow, of an icon of the Virgin Mary. Face and hands are painted, all draperies, etc., are executed in pearls.

The Midnight Mass is celebrated the night between Easter Saturday and Sunday. It lasts for about three hours, beginning at eleven o'clock at night. A bier, containing a figure representing the dead body of our Lord, is carried into the church. The bier in St. Isaak's Cathedral is of solid silver, weighs a couple of tons, and was presented by the Cossacks. It is moved on wheels. Each person on coming into the church kisses the painted hands and feet and kneels and prays for a few seconds. The Mass has begun; the church is dimly lighted. Just at midnight the priest chants" Christ is risen," the choir answers" He is risen indeed." Each kisses his neighbour, and in a moment the scene is changed from sorrow and mourning to joy and gladness. The dead Christ is carried out of the church. Chandeliers are all fitted with a piece of prepared cord running round them; this cord is fired and in a moment all the candles are alight.

Lighted tapers are put into the hands of the worshippers, a Te Deum is sung, after which all return home and eat a heavy supper.

All the food must be bought on Easter Saturday, as nothing which has been in the house during Lent can be eaten. A priest visits the houses of well-to-do parishioners and blesses all food, receiving a fee for so doing. He then goes into the markets and blesses everything which is for sale.

The supper generally consists of cold roast veal, ham, chickens, hard-boiled eggs, various kinds of cakes all decorated with bunches of paper flowers bought at the Verba, and wine, and quass, which is a kind of cider. They say that blessed food cannot do one any harm, so it may be their faith which keeps the people from indigestion, certainly I have seen dyspeptic people eat heartily of this supper and suffer no inconvenience. It seems that the mind has great influence over the body, and the meal is eaten with much joy and laughter. In workshops the proprietor prepares the supper and offers it to his employees.

The Greek Church orders that no service should be held on Easter Sunday; however, the church bells ring all day. Many Russian people go on Easter Sunday to the English and Lutheran churches.

During Easter week the Russian never goes out without a hard-boiled and coloured egg in his pocket. On meeting an acquaintance he says" Christ is risen," the answer comes, they then kiss each other three times and exchange eggs. The shops are all closed for that week except for a couple of hours in the morning, and everyone makes holiday. On Easter Monday the ceremony of greeting the troops is held in the Winter Palace. In one of the great halls the soldiers, numbering about five thousand, are drawn up. The Emperor advances, shakes hands, and says, "Christ is risen," the soldier replies; the Emperor kisses him three times, and the man then advances to the Empress, kisses her hand, presents a hard-boiled egg and receives from her a painted porcelain one. He then files out of the room, and another takes his place. So it goes on until they have all personally saluted the Emperor and Empress. It is very wearisome. On Easter Sunday the Emperor kisses all the men of his household, and the Empress kisses all the women.

One day during Eastertide we were out driving on the Nevski Prospect, and the little Grand Duchess Olga was not good. I was speaking to her, trying to induce her to sit down quietly, when suddenly she did so, folding her hands in front of her. In a few seconds she said to me, "Did you see that Policeman?" I told her that was nothing extraordinary, and that the police would not touch her. She replied, "but this one was writing something; I was afraid he might have been writing. I saw Olga, and she was very naughty." I explained that this was very unlikely, and she reminded me, rather reproachfully, that one day, sometime before, she had seen a drunken woman arrested in the street, and had wished me to tell the police not to hurt her. I had refused to interfere, saying that the woman was naughty and the police quite right in taking her. I now explained that one had to be quite big and very naughty indeed before the police would take one to prison. On returning home she made particular inquiries as to whether a policeman had come while she was out. When she went to see her parents that afternoon she recounted the whole story to her father, telling him that I said it was quite possible to live without going to prison. She then asked her father if he had ever been a prisoner; the Emperor answered that he had never been quite naughty enough to go to prison. Her remark then was: "Oh! How very good you must have been, too."

We stayed about two days in St. Petersburg and then returned to Tsarskoe Selo. Spring comes on so quickly in Russia that on our return the whole country was green and lovely, the birds were singing and every place was glorious with the beauty of spring time.

The wife of Alexander II loved cowslips. She imported some from Germany and had them planted in the park at Tsarskoe Selo. They throve very well and are now found as far away as Peterhoff, which is about thirty miles on the other side of St. Petersburg. The French call them the cuckoo flower, and both French and Swiss have a great love for the pretty, fragrant, yellow flower. A Swiss told me once that he considered it the most poetic flower that blows. There are no primroses in Russia. The climate is too dry for them. Attempts have been made to naturalise them, but without success.

We stayed at Tsarskoe Selo till early in May, when we went to Peterhoff, the summer residence in the Gulf of Finland. Here there are many Imperial residences and a great palace used for state occasions. The park is bounded on one side by the tideless Baltic. On the horizon is Kronstadt, surrounded by its forts. There is a little church of England, and "a chaplain lived there during the summer months and worked among the sailors. Kronstadt is the second strongest place in the world, and until quite lately was considered impregnable for six months of the year on account of the ice. However, the ice breakers have altered all that. The strongest place in the world is, of course, Gibraltar.

The little Grand Duchesses went to church regularly from the time they were babies. It was during this year that the Grand Duchess Olga began to notice what was said there. She came home one day and told me "the priest prayed for mama and papa, and Tatiana and me, the soldiers and the sailors, the poor sick people, and the apples and pears, and Madame G." I exclaimed at this last, so she said: "But I heard them say 'Marie Feodorovna.'" I said I thought they meant her grandmamma. She said, "No, Amama's called Amama, and your Majesty, but not Marie Feodorovna." I said "and also Marie Feodorovna," but she now replied "no one has more than two names, and I am quite sure Madame G. would be very much pleased if she knew that the priests prayed for her in church."

In Peterhoff during the hot June weather the little Grand Duchess Marie was born. She was born good, I often think, with the very smallest trace of original sin possible. The Grand Duke Vladimir called her "The Amiable Baby" for she was always so good and smiling and gay. She is a very fine and pretty child, with great, dark-blue eyes and the fine level dark brows of the Romanoff family. Lately speaking of the child, a gentleman said that she had the face of one of Botticelli's angels. But good and sweet-tempered as she is, she is also very human, as the following stories will show. When she was a very little child, she was one day with her sister in the Empress's boudoir, where the Emperor and Empress were at tea. The Empress had tiny vanilla-flavoured wafers called biblichen, of which the children were particularly fond, but they were not allowed to ask for anything from the tea table. The Empress sent for me, and when I went down little Marie was standing in the middle of the room, her eyes drowned in tears and something was swallowed hastily. "There! I've eaten it all up," said she, "you can't get it now." I was properly shocked, and suggested bed at once as a suitable punishment. The Empress said, "Very well, take her," but the Emperor intervened, and begged that she might be allowed to remain, saying, I was always afraid of the wings growing, and I am glad to see she is only a human child." She was constantly held up as an example to her elder sisters. They declared she was a step-sister. Vainly I pointed out that in all fairy tales it was the elder sisters who were step-sisters and the third was the real sister. They would not listen, and shut her out from all their plays. I told them that they could not expect her to stand that kind of treatment, and that someday they would be punished. One day they made a house with chairs at one end of the nursery and shut out poor Marie, telling her she might be the footman, but that she should stay outside. I made another house at the other end for baby, then a few months old, and her, but her eyes always kept travelling to the other end of the room and the attractive play going on there. She suddenly dashed across the room, rushed into the house, dealt each sister a slap in the face, and ran into the next room, coming back dressed in a doll's cloak and hat, and with her hands full of small toys. "I won't be a footman, I'll be the kind, good aunt, who brings presents," she said. She then distributed her gifts, kissed her "nieces," and sat down. The other children looked shamefacedly from one to the other, and then Tatiana said, "We were too cruel to poor little Marie, and she really couldn't help beating us." They had learned their lesson-from that hour they respected her rights in the family.

From her earliest age her love for her father has been most marked. When she was barely able to toddle she would always try to escape from the nurseries to go to papa, and whenever she saw him in the garden or park she would call after him. If he heard or saw her, he always waited for her, and would carry her for a little.

When he was ill in the Crimea her grief at not seeing him was excessive. I had to keep the door of the day nursery locked or she would have escaped into the corridor and disturbed him with her efforts to get to him. Every evening after tea she sat on the floor just inside the nursery door listening intently for any sounds from his room. If she heard his voice by any chance she would stretch out her little arms, and call "Papa, Papa," and her rapture when she was allowed to see him was great. When the Empress came to see the children on the first evening after the illness had been pronounced typhoid fever, she happened to be wearing a miniature of the Emperor set as a brooch. In the midst of her sobs and tears little Marie caught sight of this; she climbed on the Empress's knee, and covered the pictured face with kisses, and on no evening all through his illness would she go to bed without kissing this miniature.

Peterhoff is exceedingly pretty, but its beauty is chiefly man's work. There are well laid out parks and gardens, and the famous fountains, which equal, if not, as the Russians affirm, surpass in beauty those of Versailles. The Baltic is tideless and just there it is too landlocked to be anything more than a great lake; the place itself is relaxing and damp, therefore it is not satisfactory as a seaside resort.

Chapter VI: Concerning Peterhoff

PETERHOFF has also historical interests. Peter the Great loved the place, and built there two residences for himself. His ideas on this subject were very humble and the houses which contented him were very small and plain. One of these little cottages in Peterhoff is built in the Dutch style. The walls are tiled in blue and white; the kitchen contains a dresser with blue and white china, and there are many brass cooking utensils, all kept shining and bright. There are many specimens of his carving and other work. In front of the door is a fish pond in which are numbers of carp. These fish are so tamed and trained that at the sound of a bell they come swimming up to be fed.

Lately one of the rooms in this house was burned down. Two gentlemen went to the place, one of them lit a cigarette and threw away the still burning match. The woodwork of the house is naturally very old and thoroughly impregnated with turpentine, and, of course, highly inflammable; a great deal of damage was done before the fire could be got under.

The second of Peter the Great's houses is called "The Hermitage." It has a moat all round it and a drawbridge.

He disliked servants waiting in the room during meals, so he designed a large round table with an ingenious arrangement of pulleys by which each plate and dish could be removed and changed from downstairs. The table would seat about twenty people, and each place was furnished with a bell which the guest was supposed to ring when the plates required changing. The worst of the arrangement was that no table-cloth could be used, but I should think that matter would trouble Peter the Great very little; he was, after all, very much of a barbarian.

In the large park is "Mon Plaisir," the summer residence of Catherine the Great. In her days the park was a wood and here she used to chase the deer. On one occasion a poor hunted deer took refuge in the house and with his antler knocked a piece of the gilt moulding off the wall. The place is still shown to visitors. There is a very pretty little garden in front of the house with several fountains. The custodian asks the visitors most politely to sit down on a certain bench. Should you be so unwary as to do so you find yourself immediately surrounded by a shower of water. The wicked man has touched a spring and turned on a fountain which plays all-round the seat, and there you must stop until he turns it off again. It was at Peterhoff that Catherine awaited the news of her husband's murder. She had been separated from him for some time; he was a weak, dissolute young man, and the country was on the verge of a revolution. She was unscrupulous, and she arranged for his death. Opportunity was found in a drunken brawl, and he was stabbed by one of his friends, who immediately rode to Peterhoff, where he arrived early in the morning. Catherine took horse and rode to St. Petersburg, announced the death of the Emperor, and that she herself would hence forth reign. She settled the grievances of the soldiers, quelled all mutiny and rebellion, and ruled with a strong hand.

About four or five miles from Peterhoff is Subswina Datcha (my own villa), a little rococo house built and furnished in the First Empire style. The furniture alone would realise a very considerable fortune if sold in London. It is most beautiful; there are many very valuable pictures, and much really lovely china, including some great vases of beautiful old Dresden china. The house is surrounded by well wooded and excellently kept parks and gardens, among which is a pretty rose garden. It was built by order of Nicholas I, a ball was given there for his son's twenty-first birthday; they danced on a broad wooden bridge which spans the road.

One of the delights of the children was to go there to spend the afternoon and take tea, especially during hay-making time, when they would have rides in the hay-cocks, and run up and down the grassy slopes. Another great delight was to visit the farm, see the cows milked, feed the fowls, collect eggs, and fill baskets with apples. Two years ago the farmer's wife, a most amiable woman, was bringing up by hand four kittens whose mother had been killed. When the little Grand Duchesses went over in the morning on their Shetland ponies or bicycles, the kittens were always brought out, four bottles of milk were produced and each child, bottle of milk in one hand and a kitten comfortably tucked under her arm, would quietly take a place in the milk-cart and go for a drive round the farm-yards, feeding the kittens in the meantime.

When the Grand Duchess Marie was a baby we went to spend a day at Robshai. There were manoeuvres going on at that time to which the

28

Emperor and Empress went, and one day we drove off in a carriage drawn by four horses abreast, and after two hours fast driving we reached Robshai. The palace is large but is seldom occupied, and there are nice gardens. A short time afterwards we spent a few days at Krasnoe Selo, where there were also manoeuvres. Krasnoe Selo means "The Pretty Village" - a misnomer, if ever there was one. It is a miserable collection of dirty wooden huts, each standing a little way back from the road and with a pool of stagnant water standing before it. No trace of a garden, not even a cabbage to be seen. There is a rather pretty little park with numbers of rowan trees, and here we used to walk every morning.

When Marie was a fortnight old she was baptised in the church in the Great Palace in Peterhoff. The ceremony, which is a most imposing one, lasted for a couple of hours, or rather more. The Empress had made arrangements for me to go into the church by a particular door and to return by the same. Accordingly, on the appointed day, clad in a white silk dress, I took my place in the carriage and was driven to the church. The Cossack who was on guard would not allow the carriage to pass; I spoke no Russian, and I thought that perhaps I might be allowed to pass in on foot. I therefore got out of the carriage. But no! he lowered his bayonet and blocked the way. There I stood in my white dress in the road, with the assembled crowd gazing at me. I did not know my way round to any other door, but at last I saw an officer whose face I knew, having seen him on guard at the palace. I made my way to him, addressed him in French and told him my dilemma. The officer was exceedingly kind and took me through the guards, and into the church itself, where the priests and bishops were assembled. They were engaged in combing out their long locks. One of them came to me and in a wonderful mixture of tongues asked me how hot the water should be. I answered him in French and English, but he did not seem to understand. I then showed him on my fingers the number of degrees, and a group of interested and excited priests prepared the font for the child. Presently in came all the invited guests - ambassadors and their wives, all in the dresses of their various courts. The little Chinese lady looked very sweet and bright. She wore a gorgeous blue-figured silk Kimono, and had a little round blue cap on her head, a red flower over one ear and a white one over the other. The Roman Catholic church was represented by a cardinal with his red hat and soutane, and the head of the Lutheran

Church in Russia was also present, wearing a black gown with white ruffles. The Poles are for the most part Roman Catholic, and the Finns Lutheran or Reformed church. There were also present the suites of the various courts. The Dowager and young Empress have five hundred ladies belonging to their court - "Demoiselles d'honneur" as they are called. These ladies all dress alike on such occasions, in scarlet velvet trains embroidered in gold, with petticoats of white satin. While the elder ladies, "Les dames de la cour," wear dark green, embroidered in gold.

When all were assembled, the small heroine was carried into the church by Princess Galitzin, the senior lady of the Court. She carried a pillow of cloth of gold, on which reposed the little Marie Nicolaivna in the full glory of her lace robes lined with pink silk, and wearing a little close-fitting cap or bonnet. The Emperor, the Dowager Empress, the other god-parents and all the Grand Dukes and Duchesses and foreign royalties followed. According to the law of the Russian Church the parents are not allowed to remain in the church during the baptism, so the Emperor, having received the congratulations of his relations, withdrew from the church, returning afterwards for the Confirmation, and to bestow the Order of St. Anne upon his little daughter. The baby was then undressed to her little shirt, which was the same that the Emperor had worn at his baptism. It was, alas! stolen from the church that day and never recovered. She was then dipped three times in the font, the hair was cut in four places, in the form of a cross. What was cut off was rolled in wax and thrown into the font. According to Russian superstition the good or evil future of the child's life depends on whether the hair sinks or swims. Little Marie's hair behaved in an orthodox fashion and all sank at once, so there is no need for alarm concerning her future. The child was then brought behind the screen, where she was dressed in entirely fresh clothing, and the robe of cloth of silver was put on her and the Mass proceeded. She was again carried into the church and anointed with oil. Her face, eyes, ears, hands and feet, were touched with a fine brush dipped in oil. She was now carried round the church three times by the Dowager Empress, supported on each side by the god-fathers. Two pages held up the Empress's train. The Emperor, who had re-entered the church when the baptismal ceremony was over, came forward and invested her with her Order in diamonds, after which the procession retired in the same order that it had entered the church. The baby was brought to the church in a gilt and glass coach drawn by six snow-white horses, each horse led by a groom in white and scarlet livery with powdered wig, and she was escorted by a guard of Cossacks.

When I wished to return by the same route I had come the soldiers would not allow me to pass, I was therefore obliged to return into the church. I could not remain there, so I passed along the way I had seen the procession go, through the great state-rooms, and presently was fortunate enough to find someone from the palace. I explained my dilemma, and was left in charge of an elderly respectable woman, who I afterwards found was one of the servants of the palace, and my guide said he would telephone for a carriage. The carriage, however, did not arrive, and to return on foot was out of the question, for one thing the distance was too great, and I know enough Russian to ask a policeman. At about half-past three the woman went off to find someone to help me; she soon returned with a man who said, "I no speaking English, I speaking German." I explained that I spoke neither German nor Russian. The question of language, however, did not trouble my Good Samaritan. He called an izvochik, as the street carriages are called in Russian, put me into it and sent me home, as he imagined. I was taken to the Dowager Empress's palace by mistake at first, and when at last I arrived home I had been away in all seven hours, and now felt rather tired and hungry.

The next morning the news reached Peterhoff of the death of the Czarovitch, George Alexandrovitch. This poor young fellow had suffered from consumption for many years. He had lived for some time in Egypt, and had tried many other climates, but only at Abbas Tuman, in the Caucasus, could he breathe. His life there was lonely and sad. His mother and sisters, the Grand Duchesses Olga and Xenia, with the latter's children, used to visit him every year, going after Easter and staying until the weather got too hot for them. For the climate is hot, and the journey long and difficult, especially for children. That year, on account of little Marie's birth, the journey had been postponed till later than usual, and the poor young Grand Duke was awaiting their arrival with impatience. In a letter written just before his death he said he longed for the sound of a woman's voice, the touch of a woman's hand, and begged his mother to come as soon as possible after the baptism. He was keenly disappointed that Marie was not a boy, as he felt the burden of his heirship almost intolerable.

Through a mistake the Emperor had named him Czarovitch, instead of Heir Apparent. In Russia this title can never be withdrawn, excepting when the bearer of it becomes Emperor. After his death the Emperor named his young brother Michael Heir Apparent. He has borne his title with great dignity and honour, but he was very glad to be relieved of it by the birth of the tiny heir, the Grand Duke Alexis, on August 12th, 1904.

On the morning following the baptism the Czarovitch had got up earlier than usual. He felt better and brighter, and, notwithstanding the remonstrance of his valet, took a ride on his bicycle. He rode down a hill, and on reaching the bottom of it suddenly fell from his bicycle. An old peasant woman going to his villa with milk, accompanied by her grandson, were the sole witnesses of the accident. She ran to his assistance, and found blood pouring from his mouth. She despatched her grandson to the villa for help, and sitting on the ground took the young Grand Duke's head in her lap, but in a few minutes he was dead. Thus on the roadside, attended by an old peasant woman, died the heir to the Russian throne. He fulfilled the saying regarding the Romanoffs, that none of them will ever die in their beds. So far as I know Nicholas I was the only one who did die in his bed. He died of pneumonia, a few days after the fall of Sevastopol. Though Alexander III died a natural death, he was sitting in a chair in the balcony when it took place.

A church has been erected over the spot where George Alexandrovitch breathed his last. The Dowager Empress with all her family went to the Crimea to meet his body, which they conveyed to St. Petersburg and laid in the Fortress Church of St. Peter and St. Paul. His tomb is attended to with loving hands, fresh flowers and plants always appear on it, and every year there is held a memorial service. This service will be held so long as any of the children of his family are alive. Such is the custom of the Russian Church. It has been said that the Grand Duke George was married to a telegraph girl. The story is absolutely untrue. He lived alone in his house in the Caucasus with his servants, except when visited by his mother and family.

A few days after his funeral the battleship Alexander III was christened. The Emperor, Empress, Dowager Empress, and other members of the family went to the ceremony. According to Russian tradition they wore white mourning, for no one attends any ceremony in

Russia in black. A sudden thunderstorm came on, and the lightning struck the flagstaff. It fell on the heads of some officers standing on deck, killing three of them, and wounding seven or eight. The ship bore the name of the Dowager Empress's husband, and she was terribly upset over it. She said it would go down in its first engagement. There was another curious prophecy, that from the time it was put into action three years, counting one year for each person killed, would see the end of the Romanoff family.

Chapter VII: Concerning Father John

IN the autumn of that year we went abroad. Starting from Peterhoff, we went in the small yacht, the Alexandra, to Kronstadt, where we got on board the Standard. Father John, of Kronstadt, came on board to bless the Emperor and Empress and the children; he also blessed me. Father John has a most interesting personality; he is a kind of latter-day saint. He has written a book called" My Life in Christ," which is rather like "The Imitation of Christ." He has worked many cures, especially in paralysis, epilepsy, and other diseases of the nerves. He knows his own limitations, however, and if called upon to cure such diseases as scarlatina, diphtheria, etc., says "The disease must run its course; I can only pray for the patient." He was once called in to see a little child who was very ill with pneumonia. He brought with him some holy water, of which a little was spilt on the floor. A sister of the little sufferer was called and obliged to go on her knees, and with her tongue lick up the spilt drops. In this case Father John said he could only pray. The child eventually did recover. Some people, especially doctors, say that he is a natural hypnotist; others, that he is a faith healer. In either case, he certainly has great power over nerve diseases, and these are often the most difficult to cure. I once suggested to the Empress that he was probably simply a natural hypnotist, who had practised his powers; however, she was not pleased with the suggestion. Both she and the Emperor look upon these occult sciences with grave suspicion. The Empress says if there is anything in them at all, it is the work of the devil, and is the witchcraft spoken of in the Bible.

A doctor told me the following story: Princess B., a girl of fourteen years, the daughter of wealthy parents, was staying in the Crimea when she was suddenly struck with paralysis. He was called but could do nothing. Doctors were brought from St. Petersburg, Berlin, and Paris, and many treatments were adopted without success, and all hope of a cure was abandoned. It suddenly struck my friend that a hypnotic suggestion might possibly be of service, so he went to urge this new idea upon them. To his surprise he found they had gone to Kronstadt, taking their daughter with them. Two days after he was invited to go to see his former patient, and was delighted to find her able to walk about. This was more than fifteen years ago, and the cure has proved permanent. She is now a married woman with little children. The doctor in question is a Lutheran, and he says that Father John's power is only hypnotic. I incline to the belief that he works by faith, as did the Apostles of old. Many people are afraid of Father John, and there are many curious stories of him. It is said that he has no sympathy, no feeling, for anyone outside of the Greek Church. He is not always beneficent, as the following story will show. A young man fell into bad health, and his doctor pronounced his illness heart disease, which was incurable. He came a long distance to see Father John, who told him frankly that he must die. He said he would give him a little present which he was to open on a certain date. "On the same morning," he continued, "you will receive by post from me a small present." Father John left the room and returned with a parcel, which he handed to him with strict injunctions to lay it on one side until the stipulated date. Then he prayed with the poor sufferer and sent him away. On the morning of the appointed day the young man opened the parcel, and found it contained a shroud. He was much shocked, and was still holding the ghastly present in his hand, when the promised posted parcel was handed to him. He opened it eagerly, and found inside corpse candles - as the lights which burn round a dead body in Russia are called. The unfortunate young man dropped dead. This was surely a cruel abuse of his powers, whatever they may be. I never saw Father John again.

We started from Kronstadt in the beautiful yacht Standard. It is as large as an ocean liner, and carries a crew of five hundred men. We were followed by an escort - the Polar Star. It was in this yacht the Emperor made his voyage round the world when he was Czarovitch.

Orders had been given that in case of fog, which is very common in the Baltic, both vessels should steam at half speed. A fog came on, and the Standard reduced speed, but the Polar Star did not. She quickly overtook us and was within a few inches of our stern before she was perceived. There was a great commotion on board both vessels, and each was quickly turned a little out of her course. The Polar Star passed us so closely that we could have shaken hands with those on her decks. The rest of our voyage was accomplished without incident.

On landing at Copenhagen we were met by the old King of Denmark, the then Princess of Wales, Princess Victoria, the King of Greece, and many other royalties, and drove to Bernstorff Castle, a short distance from Copenhagen. It is a very small residence and was most uncomfortably crowded. There is a tiny park and a rose garden which the late queen had planted.

Princess Victoria took great delight in her small cousins, and they, on their part, manifested much affection for "Auntie Toria," as they always called her. Indeed, the three little girlies were objects of adoration to all the family. The Princess of Wales slept in the room adjoining mine.

Copenhagen manufactures really beautiful china. Each piece is painted by artists, and no two pieces are exactly alike. For the most part it is white and blue, and one wonders at the variety of designs which can be executed in these colours. I saw no poverty in Copenhagen, nor, indeed, any great show of riches. The people, so far as I could judge, are well educated and many of them, even amongst the servants, spoke Danish, and either English or German. They do not seem to be ashamed or afraid of work, and they are very good agriculturists and gardeners.

We spent about sixteen days in Denmark, then went on to Kiel to visit the Empress's sister, Princess Henry of Kiel. She had at this time two children. Kiel is a rather dirty, very busy little town, with a thriving port; there are, however, nice shops. If you ask a Kiel person what you can buy as a souvenir, he will always suggest smoked and cured fish. The smoking and drying form quite an extensive trade, and some hundreds of persons are employed in a factory. The fish is greatly prized all over Germany.

We stayed two days in Kiel, and then went by train to Darmstadt, or rather Wolfsgarten. On the way I noticed fields of the saffron crocuses, and I am told that saffron-growing forms quite an extensive commerce in the south of Germany. We were met at the station at Wolfsgarten by the Grand Duke and Duchess of Hesse and their little daughter, the Princess Ella, and the Duchess's sister, the Crown Princess of Roumania, a very beautiful woman. Little Princess Ella was then four years old, a sweet and pretty child, with wide grey-blue eyes and a profusion of dark hair. She was like her mother, not only in face, but also in manner. She was very much interested in her cousins, and had herself put some of her toys in their room for them, and they were soon great friends. She very much wished she had a sister of her own, and begged hard that the Grand Duchess Tatiana might be adopted as her little sister. She said we would not miss her so much as we would Olga or the baby. That prospect falling through, she made inquiries about the baby, and came to the conclusion that she and Miss W. could easily manage her. With anxious eyes she followed all the details of the baby's toilette till she thought she had mastered them. She then asked her aunt about giving it to her, and, of course, was refused. She then tried diplomacy, and kept constantly assuring us that it was a very ugly baby, and we would be much better and happier without that stupid little thing. At last she thought she had attained her object, and suggested that as the baby was so entirely horrible I should throw it away!

We spent about six or seven very happy weeks at Wolfsgarten, and had many simple pleasures, such as gipsy teas. We went twice to Darmstadt, took tea at the Palace, and went shopping with the children. Darmstadt is a well-built town, with clean open streets and nice shops. We took the children to a toy shop, and they were told that they might choose what they liked for themselves, and also for relations and friends at home. Olga looked at the things, and finally chose the very smallest she could find, and said, politely, "Thank you very much." Vainly the shop people showed her more attractive toys; she always replied: "No, thank you; I don't want to take it." I took her on one side and asked her why she would not buy the toys. I said that the people would be very sad if she would not take more, and that she could not leave the shop without buying more. So she said: "But the beautiful toys belong to some other little girls, I am sure; and think how sad they would be if they came home and found we had taken them while they were out." I explained to her, and she and Tatiana laid in a large stock.

Chapter VIII: A Glimpse of Poland

WE were very sorry to leave Darmstadt. On our way to Poland we paid a visit to Potsdam, to the German Emperor and Empress. On arriving we found the troops drawn up in a line, and the Emperor himself met us at the station. The band played the Russian National Anthem, and the two Emperors walked along and inspected the regiments. The Emperor of Russia shook hands with the officers and congratulated them. He and the Empress then went off to lunch at the palace, but we stayed in the train till after lunch, when a carriage arrived and took us up to the palace.

The German Emperor is very like his portraits; the Empress is a fine, handsome woman; she was plainly dressed in a green cloth costume. Both of them admired my little charges and took particular notice of their costumes, which were new from London for the occasion. They wore thick cream-coloured silk coats trimmed with beaver, and had hats to match, and they did look very dainty and sweet. Underneath they had cream-coloured guipure lace-frocks over pink silk, and pink sashes. We were taken upstairs by the little princess, only daughter of the German Emperor, a very sweet and nicely-mannered child. The nurseries were all sea green and silver, very attractive rooms. Here we had tea with the little prince and princess. There was no servant in the room, and the little prince himself handed round bread and butter to everyone. Tea over, they took little cousin Olga for a drive in their pony-cart, and the English nurse sent for a carriage and took the other two children and me for a drive through the famous Sans Souci grounds. We then returned to the train and got our little charges to bed. About ten o'clock the Emperor and Empress came; the train, which had been put into a siding to wait, was brought into the station; the band played, and off we started for Poland.

In Poland we stayed in a small palace called Skernivitsi. It is situated in what I should suppose to be the dirtiest little Jewish town in the world. Almost all the inhabitants are Jews, handsome, melancholy looking men; the children and young girls are lovely, while the older women are fat, coarse, untidy looking creatures. It seemed to me they wore wigs made of horse-hair, so coarse and unnatural did their hair appear. The country round was very flat and ugly, not even a hedgerow to be seen, only here and there a few trees. The Poles are for the most part Roman Catholics; at every cross road is a little shrine or altar, fenced in with iron bars. Here and there on a tree hangs a holy picture, very often much defaced with rain and weather. Going along the roads every now and again one came to a tall black cross, with a tiny figure, perhaps five or six inches long, of the Saviour of mankind hanging on it. So far as I could judge on my three visits to the country, the Poles are the most dishonest, the most untruthful, and the dirtiest people on the face of the earth. Their thefts were very extraordinary; they even pilfered the Imperial luggage when it was standing in the station.

Skernivitsi has a rather romantic history. The Emperor Paul had three sons - Alexander I, Constantine, and Nicholas I. Constantine was Viceroy of Poland; he fell in love with a Polish countess, who was, from all accounts, both beautiful and amiable, and who lived with her uncle, the Archbishop of Poland, at Skernivitsi. In order to marry her Constantine renounced his claim to the throne, though he was heir apparently, as his brother, Alexander I, though married, had no children.

On the death of her uncle it was found that he had left his niece, Skernivitsi, with its large estates and vast woods. Constantine had no children, and on his death he left the place to his brother Nicholas I. Constantine was popular with the Poles, partly, perhaps, on account of his Polish wife. Russian people will tell you that both Alexander and Constantine were childless as a direct punishment from God for the murder of their father. A life use of Skernivitsi was granted by Alexander II to Prince Baratenski in recognition of some service. On his death, a short time before we went there, the place returned to the Imperial family. The house was in bad repair, and the park a damp, gloomy place, with low-lying ponds in it; the woods teemed with game. There were lovely little black deer, with branching antlers, roebucks and fallow deer; also quantities of pheasants and partridges, to say nothing of foxes. Five or six thousand head of game was a common enough bag after one day's shooting! Foxes are shot in Russia! They do not trouble to shoot rabbits, nor do they eat them, and the people look disgusted if you say they are nice. When the game was brought home it was arranged on the lawn, sometimes with the interlaced monograms of the Emperor and Empress, sometimes with the double-headed eagle of Russia, or something distinctly Polish would be chosen. Torches were then lit and the foresters played their band. The house party then came out to view the game and talk over the incidents of the day's sport. It was a very quaint and pretty sight.

We stayed there a few days and then returned to Tsarskoe Selo, back to the ice and snow, where we remained until the new year.

Chapter IX: The Rough Life of the Russian Peasantry

I HAD now been about ten months in Russia, and had seen and learned much regarding the peasants. In most cases their marriages are arranged by the parents, and the ceremony usually takes place before the man is called upon for his military services. Boys and girls, aged respectively sixteen and fourteen years, will be married; the girl then lives with her mother-in-law and helps with the farm work, etc. Housework seems to be cut down to the lowest level. The mother prepares the food and the warm water for the weekly bath, for all peasants take a bath every Saturday night.

A Russian cabin consists of about two rooms; one has a stove, a table, a wooden bench, and a couple of chairs, a lamp, or not, according to their means. Failing a lamp, home-made candles are burned. The inner room is often destitute of furniture.

The father and mother sleep on the top of the stove with as many of the children as can be fitted there. The others take pillows and lie on the floor in their clothing.

The father and mother have supreme power over sons and daughters, daughters-in-law and grand-children, and they are all brought up together. I have counted as many as twenty-one little children all in one cabin, and have been told that there are often more. The Russian peasant receives from his proprietor a strip of land, more or less according to the number of sons in the family. In return he and his family give so many days' work to the proprietor. Boys are, therefore, very much prized; girls are less thought of, though the latter do the hardest part of the work. I have seen a woman yoked to a plough in company with the family cow, and driven by a man. In Russia women mow the rye and grass, and do many things which in this country are considered man's work.

The overcrowding of the cabins is one cause of the frightful mortality amongst Russian children. In all classes taken together some 35 per cent of the children die. It often leads to many strange diseases of which the doctors know little or nothing, as their studies are carried on in St. Petersburg or Moscow, where different conditions prevail. But I must here say that as a rule Russian doctors are very kind, and do their best for the poor people; but the country is so under-populated that one doctor has to do duty for three or four villages. He lives in the largest village, and can only visit the others at intervals of a fortnight or so. Should an epidemic break out, the doctor telegraphs to one of the universities or hospitals for someone to aid him. This help is not always forthcoming as the "Lock-outs" in the universities are frequent. The doctor then goes to the stricken village, organises a kind of hospital with such assistance as he can get, and fights the enemy, not always with success. In a village lately there was an outbreak of some infectious disease, such as diphtheria. The doctor died, and 99 per cent. of the children were swept away.

Children are the great want in Russia; the death-rate comes so close to the birth-rate, and the victims are usually those of the poorer classes. From this point of view the war in the East, with the losses of hundreds of thousands, is a terrible calamity for Russia.

For want of population, or, perhaps, I should say, for the want of the proper division of the people, many of Russia's natural advantages are untouched. There are great tracts of country almost untilled; mines in the south almost unworked; trackless forests, where rove wild animals, but which contain vast possibilities of wealth. Russian peasants will not live in solitary farm-houses, and sometimes live forty miles away from their work. In summer they simply shut up the cabin and camp on the farm, driving the beasts before them. In the autumn, when rye and oats are sown, down comes the snow, and all is kept warm; the peasant then returns to his hut for the winter.

The women do most exquisite needlework. Should there be a railway line anywhere near the village, the men are employed for a few hours each day keeping the line clear of snow. Sometimes the younger men go into the nearest town and work in the factories, or in keeping the streets clean, but they live very near starvation in many cases.

There are no shops in a Russian village; each household produces enough for its own wants, with the exception of tea, sugar, paraffin, etc. The people can make their own shoes out of strips or bark plaited together, and put on a wooden sole. Instead of stockings they wear bandages, and they are most skilful in arranging these. During war time even the officers wear these bandages; they say they march better, and should a hole come in the heel they have only to move the bandage a little and it is all right.

Such articles as cannot be produced at home are provided at the annual fair which is held in every village in spring and autumn. Men come round to each village twice a year to buy all the lace, drawn thread-work, etc., which the women have done in the intervals of farm-work. These are taken to St. Petersburg and Moscow, and sold at a large profit. The Empress wished to establish some time ago in London and other centres work depots which would give the workers a better chance of realising good prices for the products of their toil.

Chapter X: Searching for the Magic Bloom

No life is without its compensations, and life in a Russian village has its bright side also. During the long winter evenings a professional story-teller comes round. He is kept and fed at the expense of the villagers, and in return he tells them wonderful tales about gnomes, pixies, and fairies in general. Or he will relate some historical tale, or even make and recite poetry to them. Russian poetry is in blank verse, and deals very often with heroic deeds. The Russian fairy, like its Irish prototype, is, as a general rule, a malignant being, always ready to do some mean or nasty trick; but the traditions regarding them differ in many respects. The Irish peasant will tell you that after the great war in heaven, when Satan was thrown out, there fell also with him many evil spirits. The worst of these evil spirits fell at once into hell, there to remain for evermore, but those who were less guilty got another chance and fell on the earth, where they may, by their good or evil deeds, ultimately work out their salvation or damnation.

Sometimes unaccountable bruises appear on one's body, these they regard with great horror; they are supposed to be the work of evil spirits who wish to get you out of the house. In Ireland these bruises are called "dead men's pinches." So in both countries a mystical origin is given to them. One class of Russian fairies inhabits the pools and streams of fresh water, and are specially to be found in wooded spots. The Russian peasant, wandering near, hears the sound of sweet singing; should he try to distinguish the sounds his name will be called aloud. If he is so unguarded as to answer, the wicked fairies throw themselves upon him and cry, "Thou art my beloved." He is drawn down into the water and returns no more. In both countries, should you be so unfortunate as to sneeze three times, unless someone calls out "God bless you," you are indeed in a perilous situation, for the fairies will surely have you then.

Twice a year the ferns blossom; they bear a large golden flower, gifted with the power of making the fortunate finder wealthy for life. One of these nights is midsummer night; the other, the Eve of the Feast of the Assumption. All through those two nights the peasants walk in the woods searching for the magic bloom. No one has succeeded in yet finding it, for the fairies are always on the look-out, and either throw dust into the eyes of the seekers, or divert their attention to something else, and break down the flower.

As might be supposed, fire plays an important part in their superstitions. In a peasant's house the fire is never allowed to go out. Should it by chance do so, there is great dismay, as the little old man who lives behind the chimney might be offended, or might even feel the cold and die. If the family move to another home, some of the fire is taken in a small saucepan or jar packed into a basket, and is sent on by a special messenger before the rest of the family follow. When it is placed on the hearth stone the fire genius is addressed somewhat as follows: "There, grandfather, rest easy, and be assured that your place will always be the warmest in the cabin." Should the fire go out, it shows that the spirit is displeased, and all sorts of dire calamities may be expected. When the house is locked up for the summer the fire is carried in the cart in a saucepan and attended to most assiduously.

Dreams are very much regarded, and interpreters of them are held in great respect. Many people will not take any important step in life without consulting the cards; fortune- tellers must reap a large fortune. I very often had my fortune told, and strange to relate a part of what was said always came true. At Christmas many are the chances taken to see what your future will be. Some of these I had already seen practised in Ireland. On a table seven saucers are arranged in a row. Under one is placed a ring; one is left without anything, a piece of white cloth in another, earth in another, a red cloth in another, a button, and a nut, and so over all the saucers is placed a cloth. These things signify marriage, no change, a parson, death, a soldier, an engagement, and a long journey. You are sent out of the room while the saucers are being arranged; then you are blind-folded and led up to the table, told to lift the cloth and put your hand into one. According to what you find will your future be. If you go into a room just at midnight and sitting between two mirrors gaze steadily into one, you are supposed to see gradually forming on the face of the glass a picture, significant of your fate for the coming year. On midsummer night all unmarried girls go into the fields and gather seven different wild flowers. To sleep with these under the pillow is to insure a vision of her future husband.

There are many gipsies in Russia, and at Peterhoff I often witnessed their most extra ordinary marriage ceremony. Sunday is usually the day chosen for it. They choose a spot where they can drive round in a circuit. The bride and bridegroom - the bride gorgeously dressed in a new print or muslin dress, a pair of white cotton gloves, and a piece of lace shaped like a three-cornered handkerchief with the corner hanging down behind, tied over her head and crowned with a wreath of artificial flowers take their places in a little pony-cart. After them come the groomsmen and bridesmaids, who are dressed like the bride, but without the crowning glory of the wreath, two in each cart; then the elders of the camp, the grave married people generally accompanied by a few children, and, last of all, the bachelors or widowers. This strange procession drives round the chosen route three times and the marriage is accomplished. It holds good and is quite legal. I suppose the presence of so many witnesses makes it so.

There are many ceremonies of blessings observed by the Russians. I have already spoken of blessing the food on Easter Saturday. On the first of July (old style) the apples and orchards generally are blessed, and the very worst boy in the village would not steal an apple before it had been blessed. After the blessing the fruit is offered for sale in the streets and market-places. After the ice has melted the fishing-boats are all blessed before they go to sea.

Chapter XI: A Russian Christmas

WE generally spent Christmas at Tsarskoe Selo. It is less observed than Easter in general, but in the palace it is a great festival. There were no fewer than eight Christmas trees in various parts of the palace. The Empress dressed them all herself, and personally chose the presents for each member of her household, and for each officer, to the number of about five hundred. A tree was arrayed for the Cossacks in the riding-school. The children and I had a tree for ourselves. It was fixed into a musical-box which played the German Christmas hymn, and turned round and round. It was indeed a glittering object. All the presents were laid out on white covered tables, and the tree stood for several days an object of intense interest and admiration to the children. They were very sad when it was dismantled just before we went to St. Petersburg, but they were consoled by being allowed to help, and to divide the toys between the members of their own household.

We went to St. Petersburg on the last day of the old year (Russian counting). On New Year's Day there was a great ceremony in the palace cathedral. The Emperor and Empress and the Dowager Empress went to church in state, accompanied by their own courts and all the grand ducal courts, all wearing full court dress. We saw the Empress when she was dressed; very magnificent she looked in her court dress of white satin with its long train of brocade, seven chains of diamonds round her neck, a girdle of the same sparkling gems round her waist, the ends falling to the hem of her dress. On her head she wore the kokoshnik, the crescent-shaped head-dress, in white brocade, lavishly decorated with large single stone diamonds. A rich lace veil depended from it and hung at the back almost to her knees.

The little girlies were delighted to see her so gorgeously attired; they circled round her in speechless admiration for some time, and suddenly the Grand Duchess Olga clapped her hands, and exclaimed fervently, "Oh! Mama, you are just like a lovely Christmas tree!" After divine service was finished there was a drawing-room, at which all the debutantes were presented.

The Grand Duchesses Olga and Tatiana Nicholaivna were fond of listening to stories. On one occasion Tatiana told Olga a story, the end of which was as follows: "So my little girl and my niece went into the wood and a big wolf ate my little girl, so she went to heaven." Olga was horrified at such theology. "Oh no!" she cried; "she could not have gone to heaven, because the wolf ate her, and God does not allow wolves to go to heaven. She is walking about the wood inside the wolf." The other child calmly accepted this wonderful correction. I found I had to be very careful in telling them stories. On one occasion I told Olga the story of Joseph and his brethren. She was deeply interested, and exclaimed, "What a shame!" I said, "Yes; it was indeed a terrible shame for them to be so jealous and so cruel to their young brother." She exclaimed, "I mean it was a shame of the father. Joseph was not the eldest, and the beautiful coat should have been given to the eldest son; the other brothers knew that, and perhaps that was why they put him in the pit." Explanations were useless; all her sympathies were given to Reuben. She was angry with King David because he killed Goliath, and said, "David was much younger and smaller, and poor Goliath never expected him to throw stones at him." "Jack the Giant Killer" gave her no pleasure; it upset her idea that might was right. Once there was a cinematograph exhibition for the children and some friends. One picture showed two little girls playing in a garden, each with a table before her covered with toys. Suddenly the bigger girl snatched a toy from the little one who, however, held on to it and refused to give it up. Foiled in her attempts, the elder seized a spoon and pounded the little one with it, who quickly relinquished the toy and began to cry. Tatiana wept to see the poor little one so ill-treated, but Olga was very quiet. After the exhibition was over she said, "I can't think that we saw the whole of that picture." I said I hoped the end of it was that the naughty big sister was well punished, adding that I thought we had seen quite enough as I had no wish to see anything more of such a naughty girl. Olga then said, "I am sure that the lamb belonged at first to the big sister, and she was kind and lent it to her sister; then she wanted it back, and the little sister would not give it up, so she had to beat her."

Chapter XII: Life in the Kremlin

QUITE early in January the opening ball of the St. Petersburg season was given at the Winter Palace. Over five thousand people were present, and it was indeed a gay scene. The Empress wore white chiffon embroidered with chenille and sparkling sequins, and many diamonds. The Grand Duchess Serge wore mauve. She is sister to the Empress, and the Grand Duke was the Emperor's uncle; they have no children. The Grand Duchess Serge is a very beautiful woman; some people, indeed, even consider her handsomer than the Empress. The Imperial family was still in mourning for the Grand Duke George, so all wore either white or mauve. The ball was opened by a polonaise. The master of the ceremonies went before the Emperor and Empress, walking backwards, and cleared a way for them through the crowd. After him came Princess Galitzin, the senior lady of the Court, then came the Emperor and Empress, grand dukes and duchesses, Royal princes and princesses, the ambassadors and their wives, all moving slowly, in pairs. At the conclusion of the polonaise general dancing began. The Emperor and Empress went amongst their guests and spoke a few words to most of them. The Japanese Ambassador and his wife were there; he wore European uniform, and she was clad in a pink satin dress, made high and with long sleeves.

The supper-rooms were beautifully arranged like gardens. There were groups of palms, flowering lilacs, and laburnums, etc., appearing out of grassy beds in which grew crocuses, daffodils, and other flowering bulbs. Walks covered with carpets to imitate sand ran through the rooms in various directions; electric lamps hung in the trees and tables were set out under their shade. For the supper were provided three hundred and fifty dishes of chicken, each dish containing three chickens with salad and jelly; three hundred and fifty large lobsters, with mayonnaise sauce, and three hundred and fifty tongues and the same number of dishes of cold assorted meats, also of ices, creams, jellies, etc., besides cakes, biscuits, etc.. Also several hundred gallons of soup of various kinds. Two thousand bundles of asparagus were boiled for the salads; there were also quantities of fruit and wine. A ball at the palace is good for trade in St. Petersburg. I was invited to the kitchens to see the preparations, and was greatly amused and interested to see the people. Counts, barons, hotel proprietors, etc., all came in to see the chef and bargain with him for the remains of these delicacies. The chef is paid so much a head for the supper; he buys things in large quantities, and sends abroad for some. He orders what he likes, provides the supper, receives the money from the Emperor, and pockets what he can make out of the transaction.

Every season five or six balls are given, beside many great dinners, and twice a week there is a representation in the palace theatre, either an opera or a play, followed by a supper. It may not be generally known that the Emperor has an opera company and an acting company, which includes a ballet.

On the 6th of January the ceremony of blessing the waters is performed. A mass at which all appear in full court costume is celebrated in the Winter Palace Cathedral. That finished, the priests, in their most gorgeous vestments, followed by the Emperor and grand dukes and the gentlemen of the various courts, go to a pavilion erected over the river, and there the priests solemnly bless the waters, a hole being cut in the ice for the purpose into which a cross is lowered. They then go through the crowd which always assembles and sprinkle them from a brush dipped into the holy water. Some of the water is then brought into the palace and put into glasses reserved specially for it, and it is then drunk after many prayers and much blessing of themselves by the Russians.

Formerly, when the hole was cut in the ice, numbers of people plunged into the water, and afterwards went from door to door showing their frozen garments as a proof of their holiness, and asking alms from the charitably disposed. But from time to time one of those self-made martyrs was drowned and there were many abuses, so the authorities put an end to the plunging. The ladies of the Court used formerly to go in the procession, but bare shoulders were not exactly conducive to health with the thermometer standing often at twenty degrees below freezing point, and therefore the practice was discontinued.

We stayed at St. Petersburg until towards the end of Lent.

On one occasion the Prince of Siam came to visit the Empress, and the children were in the room. Now I was interested to see his dusky highness as I had met him before at a little seaside resort in the west of

Ireland. He had been invited to spend the summer holidays with a school-fellow, and Kilkee was chosen by his family for their holiday-resort. Some of the visitors there got up a little entertainment for the benefit of the poor, and he and his friends were invited to help. The entertainment took the form of tableaux, with a little music. The young prince was deeply interested in all, and finally begged for a part for himself. One excuse after another was offered to him, but at last to our consternation he exclaimed, "I know why you will not have me. It is because I am an Eastern. Well, I'll make a tableau all for myself." He went home and presently re-appeared with an armful of curtains, table-cloths, etc. Throwing these down in a corner of the hall, he went out again, and presently returned with all the false jewellery the village shops could supply, and announced that he intended to personate the Queen of Sheba when she had seen Solomon's magnificence. He quickly dressed the platform to represent an Eastern interior, and, draping himself in a shawl, squatted, native fashion, in the middle of the stage. It was wonderfully effective. On the evening of the exhibition the tableau was by far the finest, being so much out of the common. The boy was delighted with himself and his audience. When I saw him in the Winter Palace he was dressed in Russian uniform, and looked about him with the same bright, interested expression he had worn in Ireland. Naturally he did not recognise me. My little charges ran forward and examined him with deep interest, walking slowly round him, and regarding him with beaming smiles of amusement. The Empress said to the Grand Duchess Tatiana, "Come, shake hands with this gentleman, Tatiana." She laughed, and said, "That is not a gentleman, mama; that's only a monkey." The Empress, covered with confusion, said, "You are a monkey yourself, Tatiana," but the prince laughed heartily. They and the prince afterwards became quite good friends.

We went that year to Moscow for Easter, and stayed in the historic Kremlin. Moscow is the most characteristic city I have seen; for the most part it is distinctly modern, but conveys the impression of antiquity even more successfully than St. Petersburg does. The Kremlin and all that part are very old; there is a great room having a throne draped with ermine. All round the walls are painted frescoes. One set represents the history of Joseph and his brethren. They are dressed as Russian peasants in shirts and top-boots; Potiphar's wife is attired in a bright blue dress, showing a white petticoat. She evidently wore a crinoline, also a pair of boots with high heels and white stockings. Another set represents the wandering of the children of Israel in the wilderness; Russian costume again prevails amongst them. Another wall is taken up with the judgment of Vladimir. He was the first Christian Emperor of Russia. Tradition says that a Jew had oppressed a Christian woman, who called to Vladimir for help. The verdict went against the Jew, who straightway gave all his property to wife and children, and then said he had nothing to pay with. Vladimir ordered his head to be shaved, and that he should be mounted on a donkey and led through the town with his hands tied. He was accordingly brought out, but had not proceeded very far when he offered to refund all that he had unjustly extorted, and even more. The flies and stinging insects which abound in Russia had punished him by alighting on his shaven head.

On the floor of this room is a carpet made in a convent. It represents years of work, and it is made of pieces of cloth stitched together and bordered with fancy stitching in gold-coloured thread. On each piece is worked a regimental badge in the national colours. I thought it ugly and confusing to the eyes, but I have heard it very much admired. At the top of this room, right up under the ceiling and artfully arranged so as to be invisible from below, is a window from which the secluded women could look down upon the festivities below. Here the poor young grand duchesses used to get a peep at their future husbands. The rooms where they lived are still shown; they were bare and miserable, with the windows very high up. Poor things! Their lives must have been lamentable; they occupied themselves with needlework and much of their tapestry and cross-stitch work still exists. In a church in the Kremlin there is a carpet worked by the ladies of one of the courts. In the palace at Gatchina are tapestries representing the history of the world, beginning with the Garden of Eden and ending with Solomon's Court, also the work of the ladies of the Court.

Queen Elizabeth gave Ivan the Terrible some magnificent silver tankards and cups of beautiful workmanship, far more beautiful than any modern work, I think. This silver is all displayed in the great room I have described.

The museum is well worth a visit. Here are hung up in a circle all the crowns belonging to the various Emperors and Empresses now dead.

Catherine the Great had all the jewels of her crown picked out and made into an ornament for her personal adornment, and there hangs her crown with its jewelless holes, a lasting monument to her character. Catherine I, who was a slave girl unable to read, was far more noble in character.

There are numbers of thrones, from a little ivory chair which formerly belonged to some of the Georgian kings, to the silver one which was brought from Kieff. I sat in most of them to the great horror of some of the Russians. Some of the thrones have cords stretched across the corners to prevent such sacrilege.

Here are hung up in a glass case the robes worn by the Emperor, Empress and Dowager Empress on the occasion of their coronations. All, even to the gloves and shoes, are displayed. I should like to have retained something, if only a glove, in memory of such a momentous ceremony. In presses round the walls of another room are kept the coronation robes of former sovereigns.

Li Hung Chang brought a carved eagle to the Emperor and a screen to the Empress. The eagle is about five feet high, and stands on the carved trunk of a tree. Each feather is carved separately and can be withdrawn from the body of the bird, and the whole thing packed in a small space. It is of ivory and ebony, a most wonderful piece of work. I thought at first that the screen was painted, but it is not. It is executed with the needle, is in four panels, each representing the sea under a different aspect, while on the reverse side gulls are embroidered flying, feeding, and swimming - a truly marvellous piece of work, every part of the canvas being covered with stitches. It took eight of the most expert needlewomen in China three years to execute.

There is a collection in the museum of old state carriages - wonderful erections, all gilding and velvet, with delicately painted panels. Catherine's travelling carriage is there. There is a long table down the middle of it, and how it could be turned I know not; it is rather larger than an ordinary tramcar or 'bus. Indeed, I do not believe that there is a street in Moscow in which one of those carriages could be turned. The little Grand Duchess Olga sat in each carriage in turn; finally she selected the largest and handsomest, and said, "I'll have this one." She then gave orders quite seriously that the carriage should be sent to Tsarskoe Selo for her. She was told that could not be, so she ordered that it should be prepared for her daily drive. I was very pleased that her ideas on the subject of the carriage were not carried out.

Moscow has many picture galleries and places of interest, and the town itself is so interesting that it is well worth a visit. Moscow is particularly nice at Easter. Something in the atmosphere of the place makes it seem suitable for that festival. They say that Holy Moscow contains seventy times seven churches; as a matter of fact, there are many more, one out of every five buildings being a church. What supports them, and how the priests live, I have never been able to find out. Many of these churches are very beautiful and interesting.

As in St. Petersburg, there is a large English colony and an English church. The streets are for the most part paved with cobble stones, so they are very noisy to drive over. Some of the churches are very old, as they escaped the fire. Many of the holy icons have had almost miraculous escapes from being destroyed. One of the churches in the Kremlin contains a picture with the mark of a sword-cut like a great scar across it, but the canvas was not cut. It has also the marks of something on the back, and it is said that it was thrown out of church by the French soldiers, was put into the fire, but was miraculously preserved.

Ivan the Terrible, who was contemporary with Queen Elizabeth, had a church built which is very much admired. Seven little churches open one after the other, each round in form, six of them round a centre one. They are very pretty and full of interest, but exceedingly dark. Tradition says Ivan was much pleased with this church, and sent for the architect to reward him. When the man came, the Emperor had him seized and bound and his eyes were burned out in order that he might never be able to reproduce the church, nor to design one exceeding it in beauty. But the story is open to doubt. It is told of the designers of many famous buildings, including the cathedral at Strasburg. The church of the Assumption is very fine and well worthy of a visit.

Within the walls of the Kremlin are seven churches, many of them very interesting. In one of these the Emperor was crowned. The Emperor himself places the crown on his head, he then crowns the Empress, who kneels before him. One of the churches in the Kremlin has the highest tower in Russia. From this tower the great bell of Moscow fell, and was broken. It stands on a pedestal on the ground, at least forty men could stand under it. Since that accident the bells are fastened to the floor with padlocks and chains. I went to the top of the tower and was very glad to get down again. A short time before our visit two so-called gentlemen went up. On arriving at the top one of them drew from his pocket a little cat and threw it over the parapet. The poor little animal turned round in the air a few moments, then got up and ran away, apparently quite unhurt. It was done for a wager, of course, but it was a brutal act. Ivan the Terrible was married six times. The Russian Church allows only three marriages, and in one of the churches a place is shown just outside the consecrated part where he was obliged to sit to hear divine service with his last three wives.

I think it is in this church that the remains of Demitri the Martyr lie. He was son of Ivan the Terrible's fourth wife, and became Emperor at nine years of age. Ivan had three sons; the eldest he killed with a blow from a bar of iron; the second son became epileptic, and was therefore, by Russian law, unable to reign; little Demitri was the third son, son of the fourth wife. The brother-in-law of Feodor, second son, became Regent; his name was Boris. He found power very attractive, and tried, first of all, to usurp the throne by declaring that Demitri, being the son of the fourth wife, was illegitimate; but the people were too much attached to the old dynasty to render this possible. He accordingly induced the child's attendants to leave him unguarded for half an hour in one of the courtyards of the Kremlin. When they returned all traces of the boy had disappeared. Boris gave out that the child was epileptic, and had been placed under restraint, which seemed a probable enough story, and there were no immediate heirs to contradict it, as his sister was childless, so he usurped the throne and assumed the title of Emperor.

In later years a false Demitri arose, saying he had escaped from prison. In person he was very like the Imperial family, and his cause was taken up with great warmth, especially in Poland, to which country he said he had escaped, and he found many powerful supporters who provided him with soldiers and money. He succeeded in defeating Boris, whom he put to death, and seized the throne. He ruled neither well nor wisely, and was finally denounced by someone who seems to have known him well. The nobility took up arms against him, and his army was defeated. He threw himself from a window in the Kremlin as the nobles and their soldiers were entering to take him prisoner. Boris had had the remains of little

Demitri exhumed and re-interred in one of the churches of the Kremlin. The Russian Church canonised the little martyr to love of power.

Shortly after the death of Boris, the soldier who had killed the child and a housemaid who saw the wicked deed perpetrated, both confessed the crime. Michael Romanoff, then a boy of sixteen years, was elected by the nobility as their Emperor. His father had been viewed with suspicion and dislike by Boris, who forced him into a monastery.

Michael was a wise ruler, and soon brought order and tranquillity to reign where all had been confusion and chaos. He had also family claims upon the throne, as two of the former Empresses had belonged to the house of Romanoff.

Outside the gates of the Kremlin is a little church or shrine in which is kept the "miracle-working" image. It is guarded day and night, and priests are set aside for its sole service. Should anyone be ill and send for this image, it is placed in a carriage and guarded by two priests and taken to the house, where it is left for an hour or two; prayers are said and offerings are made, and the patient sometimes recovers. There is no specific charge made for the use of the image, but those requiring its intercession are supposed to give offerings or a present, according to their means.

The Kremlin has five gates, each one guarded by two copper-covered turrets. The copper has turned green with age and the influences of the weather, and looks very picturesque. One of these gates is the far-famed sacred gate. On it is hung a picture of our Saviour, and all who pass beneath it are bareheaded. The Russians are a very religious people, and are not ashamed of outward observances. In this they remind one of the Roman Catholics of Ireland.

At some little distance from the town is the palace in which Napoleon slept during his occupation of Moscow. In one of the yards of the Kremlin are hundreds of French cannons abandoned during the calamitous retreat from Moscow. Tolstoi says in his great work, "War and Peace," that the French were defeated not through human agency, but as the direct will of God, and laughs to scorn the idea that the general who retreated, and got the Moscow folks to fire their own residences, was actuated by military motives; he says it was all pure fate. I do not know, but almost all Russians give him credit for a far-seeing policy, and certainly the results justified his actions.

Towards the south Moscow terminates in a large red gate, known as "The Red Gate." St. Petersburg also terminates with a gate, beyond which is country. These are the only two towns I know which do so. Some way beyond the Red Gate is a pretty house and park, belonging to the Emperor, called Niskutchni; it means "sans souci"; literally, "no sadness." We often went there and had tea in the house or garden, according to weather. Snowdrops, and many flowers, grow wild here all over the grass; cowslips have been introduced and flourish well.

While we were in Moscow the Empress thought she would like to have the children's portraits painted, so an artist was engaged to paint them. They were aged at this time four years, two and a half years, and two months. He began by taking innumerable photographs of the children, then he made a collection of all existing likenesses, and then found he could not paint from photographs. He explained to me that it would not be artistic to do so. I begged him to remember what babies they were, and to work from photographs. But, no! Even to paint their frocks he insisted upon them sitting to him for three or four hours each day. Of course the poor children got very impatient, and one day the little Grand Duchess Olga lost her temper, and said to the artist, "You are a very ugly man, and I don't like you a bit." To my amazement he was exceedingly displeased, and replied, "You are the first lady who has ever said I was ugly, and moreover, I'm not a man - I'm a gentleman!" He could not understand why I laughed.

Chapter XIII: In Belovege

WE returned to Tsarskoe Selo from Moscow, and stayed there until we went to Peterhoff.

The Imperial estate in Peterhoff belongs to the reigning Empress. It is settled on her for life, and she must hand it on to the wife of the next Emperor. It belongs at present to the Dowager Empress; at her death it will pass to the Empress Alexandra Feodorovna.

The story of Peterhoff is as follows: when Nicholas I was a young man he paid a visit to the German Court. A tournament was arranged and the young Grand Duke acquitted himself bravely. Afterwards all who took part in the tournament rode up under the balcony where the ladies of the family were seated. The young princess of Prussia threw him a wreath of roses which he caught on his sword. An attachment speedily sprang up between the couple and they were married. When he became Emperor he bought what is now the private park at Peterhoff, and built a residence in it, which he named The Cottage. In memory of his first meeting the Empress said that everything in the house should bear the device of a wreath of roses on a sword.

The Dowager Empress is a very attractive person. She has the full rich voice, and the excessive tact which belong to the Danish family, as well as their youthful looks. This latter fact should not surprise us, as, according to the old story, they have the stone of youth. A Limerick man once went to stay in Copenhagen, where he found himself very comfortable - one person vied with another to make him happy. When he was going away he said to his kind entertainers, "Tell me what I can do for you; I will go to the ends of the earth to serve you." They told him that in a certain spot in a field in County Limerick a box of gold was buried. If he would dig up the box he would find a stone ring. This ring he was asked to send to Copenhagen, but for his trouble he could keep the gold.

On arriving in his own country the warm-hearted Irishman at once repaired to the field and quickly unearthed the treasure. He started off to Copenhagen, bearing the box of gold with him. He pressed his kind friends to take the box, but they insisted on retaining only the ring of stone, which they put into a safe place. They then addressed him thus: "Unfortunate wretch! you have betrayed and ruined your country. All would have gone well as long as the ring of youth remained in her, but from henceforth all poverty will leave Denmark, and her women will be always young and beautiful, while Ireland will bear a double burden of poverty, her children will be forced to other countries, nothing will thrive in Ireland."

From Peterhoff we went to Belovege, near the borders of Poland, for shooting. There is a great forest as large as the whole of Ireland; in parts it is trackless; people are often lost there, and wander round and round in a circle, cutting notches in trees as they pass them, and dead bodies are frequently found there. A few weeks before we arrived, the dead body of a traveller was found only a few minutes' walk from security.

The late Emperor had a clearing made of almost three and a half square miles, and built a small palace on a slight elevation. There are prettily laid out gardens, and the building itself is picturesque. Inside it is much decorated, and one room would delight a philatelist; it is altogether decorated with stamps - walls, furniture, everything are covered with old postage stamps. It has the effect of curious looking mosaic. I have been told that many of the stamps are very valuable specimens. The work of sticking them on alone must have been tremendous.

In the forest roam elk, bison, great red deer, and wild boars. An elk is the gentlest creature that lives, even if wounded he never attempts to turn on his assailant; the bison, however, is ferocious, as is also the wild boar. The elk is a very ugly animal, like a horned donkey. We never went into the forest without a guide, it being too dangerous. Fires frequently occur, so a very strict watch is kept for remains of fires lighted by gipsies and others passing through the forest. Forest fires are put out by cutting down trees and digging a ditch outside the fire, but they sometimes rage for days. There are many venomous snakes in the forest, therefore one must be cautious. I realised more in Belovege than anywhere else how terrible nature can be in her solitary places. The forest frightened me with its unknown possibilities of danger. I believe wild men are more to be feared there, than wild beasts. These are men who have been deprived of their passports and sent into the country.

Just before we went to Belovege there had been an outbreak of smallpox in the village and surrounding country. It was treated in what is called the Swedish method. Every patient was vaccinated seven times on successive days. The treatment was most successful; there had been two hundred and fifty cases and four of them were babies under a year old. Not a single patient died, nor were any of them disfigured by this terrible disease.

From Belovege we went to Spala in Poland for shooting. Here there is little big game, and the forest is much smaller than that of Belovege, only being about as large as Yorkshire. It is also more open; a pretty river in which boating may be had runs through the estate.

Various surprises had been arranged for the children. In a little orchard a tea-house had been built and about a dozen tame deer turned in, besides tame pheasants, hares, etc. These creatures would all come and eat from our hands, and the deer would follow me about everywhere, lay their pretty heads on my arm and, looking beseechingly in my face, seem to beg for notice. The Grand Duchess Tatiana named them "the pretty creatures" and by this name they were henceforth known. Outside the palings enclosing this fairyland flowed a river in which swam all manner of water-fowl which would come to be fed; so it was a regular paradise for children.

A further surprise awaited them in the shape of a little goat-carriage drawn by a pair of goats, each led by a boy in Polish costume, a long frock coat of white homespun decorated with black braid, and a high crowned black felt hat trimmed gaily with bands of black velvet ribbon, coloured paper flowers and a rosette of different coloured ribbons. The trimming was pinned on the hat!

Chapter XIV: The Young Officer and the Dolls

WE went to the Crimea on leaving Spala. We arrived at Alma just at bedtime, and I was disappointed not to see anything of that famous battle ground. On waking in the morning I was delighted to find we were still in the station, so I had a good look at it from the windows. We started about eight o'clock and were soon going through most beautiful country. High mountains clothed with trees, most beautiful in their autumn colouring; I never saw such foliage. Shortly afterwards we came to Inkermann. Here is a wonderful monastery hewn in the side of a great cliff. Nature made most of the caves which are used as rooms, but the monks themselves did much excavation. The windows and doors are manufactured and the monastery is well furnished and contains a very beautiful church.

Shortly after leaving Inkermann we arrived in Sevastopol. The Russians pronounce it Sevastdpol, with the accent on the third syllable. Here the yacht was awaiting us and we went on board. I am particularly fond of yachting as long as we are at anchor, but when we begin to move, it is quite a different story.

Sevastopol would appear quite impregnable, situated as it is on high barren cliffs rising straight out of the water; one wonders how the allied armies ever effected a landing. I was looking at it, thinking of these things, when Baron M., who is the general of a Cossack regiment, asked me of what I was thinking. I told him, and with a twinkle in his eyes he told me the following yarn: "You see," said he, "the poor Russians were very hungry and the cook prepared a particularly nice dinner. They all ran off when they heard the dinner bell, and the English calmly walked in, and when the Russians returned the English were waiting for their dinner inside the town. It was a great shock to the Russians." I thanked him politely for his addition to my knowledge of history, and he told me he would always be very happy to supplement my education, but that if what I heard from him was different from what I had heard, I could believe whichever I liked.

We only stayed one day at Sevastopol that time, and proceeded by sea to Yalta. The Black Sea is usually very rough and this time was no exception. The journey from Sevastopol to Yalta is about fourteen hours long; we had sailed in the night, so we arrived early next day. It was a great relief to be once more on terra firma.

Yalta is a pretty little town with a large holiday population; out of season there are very few people. The shops are shut and the owners of them start to the Caucasus or to the more remote parts of Russia, and buy or sell there. Many of the shopkeepers are Jews; some are Armenians. One shop I knew was kept by a little Armenian woman and her husband. She had been rescued by some missionaries and placed in an English mission school, where she learnt to speak English. She adored Mr. Gladstone and quite believed that he was inspired. She had a nice little shop with all manner of Eastern articles, Caucasian silver and pretty things suitable for presents. Some of these fancy trifles are very reasonable in price whilst others are more expensive than in London. Silver is, however, cheap and very quaint.

Livadia, as the Emperor's estate is called, is half-way up a mountain, and is surrounded by vast vineyards sloping down to the sea. The grapes are delicious. The Black Sea, like the Baltic, is tideless. At Livadia is a stony beach where the children played every morning. They would get on their paddling drawers and shoes, and go wading in the sun-warmed water, and gather pebbles. On one occasion I was taking them home when we met a young officer from the Standart. He asked them what they had in their hands and the children showed the little bits of green stones they had picked up, and gravely asked him to keep them if he would like to. He took a little stone from each child and when I afterwards saw them they were mounted in gold and attached to his watch chain. He said he would not part with them for any earthly consideration, the children having found them themselves, and offered them to him. Indeed, it was very amusing to see the way in which people regarded these little maidens. On one occasion we were getting into the carriage at Peterhoff when an officer came running over to say good morning. The little Grand Duchesses, who were friendly creatures, began to talk to him, and one of them took a little wooden toy from her pocket and asked him if he would like it. He was much pleased and afterwards turned to me and said he was in trouble, and seeing the children coming out, thought that if he could reach the carriage in time to bow to the children he would find a way out of his troubles. "And see," said he, "not only did I bow to them but I kissed their hands and received a little toy from one of them. I shall keep that toy as long as I live." When next I met him he told me the omen had been verified, and he had found a way out of his trouble.

There was a tall young German officer in the Guards, and he used to ask the Grand Duchess Olga for a doll; a little tiny one that he could keep in his pocket and play with while he was on guard would give him much pleasure, so he declared. Poor little Olga Nicolaivna did not know if he was joking or in earnest. I told her I was sure the doll would give him much pleasure, and that it should be a very small one. She presently brought me a couple of very tiny dolls dressed as boys, one minus a foot, the other without an arm. I said I thought it would be better to give unbroken dolls, and she replied, "Yes, but these are boys and he is a man, I am afraid he would not like a little girl dolly." I then told her to ask him when she saw him.

Next morning the doll was put into her pocket and in the course of our walk we met Captain S., who immediately began to reproach her for having forgotten how lonely he was and what company a little doll would be to him. She plunged her hand into her pocket and produced the doll, holding it behind her back. "Which would you rather have," she said seriously, "a boy or a girl doll?" He answered, quite seriously, "A little girl doll would be like you, and I should love it very much, but a boy would be very companionable." She was quite delighted and gave him the doll, saying, "I am glad, I was so afraid you would not like the girl." He put the doll away most carefully.

Shortly afterwards the young officer went for his holidays. When he returned, the first day he saw the little Grand Duchess he began as formerly to beg for a doll. She said reproachfully, "Is it possible you have already broken the nice little doll I gave you?" With great tact he explained that the little doll was lonely all by itself, and wanted a companion, and that it did not matter if it was broken; so another dolly was carried about for several days till she met him again and gave it to him.

The sun-warmed sea looked very tempting, and I thought I should like to bathe in it, but I had no bathing-dress. I accordingly sent one of the under-nurses to Yalta to get one, either a ready-made costume or stuff to make one. When she returned she said the only thing she could find was a Russian peasant's red cotton shirt, and she supposed I would not like that. I was quite of the same opinion, but asked if she had been able to get serge or galatea of which I could make a costume. She told me she had gone into a shop where they sold stuffs and asked for something to make a bathing dress. The woman asked her if it was for herself, and she replied that it was for another person. The shopkeeper turned scornfully upon her and said: "Bathing dress, indeed! French fashions! Tell her to go and bathe in her skin as her grandmother did before her."

At Massandra, half-way up a mountain at the other side of Yalta, is a delightful rose garden. The roses look like two walls, one at each side of the path. At the back are reve d'ors, trained on espaliers; they attain a height of seven or eight feet. In front of them are dwarf specimens in all colours and shades, down to tiny pink and white trees not more than a foot in height. All the ground at the foot of those rose trees is carpeted with violets. In the background stand cypresses like grave sentries. I got to love the cypress, while it is green, but no tree looks half so ghostly, when it is dead. There are many tropical plants and trees in this lovely garden. Deodars from the Himalayas, monkey-puzzles as large as forest trees, great magnolias, and many others of which I did not know the names. Higher up the mountain is a second rose garden. Here the roses are trained to grow along wires stretched horizontally about a foot from the ground. The effect is as of sheets of flowers. There is a great bed of La France roses, another of yellow roses in all shades, and still another of mixed red, pink and white roses. These beds were each at least one hundred feet long by perhaps seventy wide. This garden is also enclosed by stately cypresses looking like sentries mounting guard.

At Aloupka, on the Livadia side of Yalta, is a beautiful residence. There is an avenue of mangolias stretching for about a mile, a lovely sight when the trees are covered with white blossoms, the perfume of which is delicious.

The entrance to the house is very imposing, great flights of white marble steps with beautifully sculptured lions on each landing. The property round this fine house has fallen into terrible decay. I never saw anything like the neglected state of the fields. Nothing one could see but weeds and stone though all around are well cultivated fields and tobacco farms, paying very well.

It seems the proprietor of Aloupka is still a minor; he inherited when he was a baby. His mother and trustees sold the farms to the peasants, who certainly have neglected their holdings. The young proprietor lives abroad and I am told is unable to speak even a word of Russian.

Both the inside of the house and gardens are in habitable order. I have been told that the boy possesses a great estate in the Black Earth district, so when he is grown he may return to Russia and make acquaintance with his own people.

The next property to Livadia is Orianda. It formerly belonged to the Grand Duke Constantine, but the Emperor recently bought it. Unfortunately the house was burned down seven years ago and has never been rebuilt. I expect it will be prepared for the Ozarovitch when he is grown up. Little except the foundations remain.

There is a little church on the property the belfry of which is a great oak tree. Here the bells are suspended from the boughs, a platform has been erected with a flight of steps leading up to it. The great bell is only rung in cases of fire.

The grounds of Orianda are very pretty and we frequently took tea there. There are shallow basins in the grounds with goldfish. When we returned to the Crimea two years after, the goldfish had disappeared. I asked what had become of them. The man said, "Alas! we wanted to clean out their little lakes, so with great care we captured the goldfish and put them into the large pond in which the swans live, but we could not find them again." "No," said I, "of course not, the swans ate them." He held up his hands and exclaimed in horror: "Oh no, Miss, those swans are particularly tame; his Majesty takes great notice of them; they would never eat anything that belonged to the Emperor."

Beyond Orlanda is Ai Toder, or St. Theodore's, the residence of the Grand Duke Alexander who is married to the Emperor's sister, the Grand Duchess Xenia Alexandrovina. They have five sons and a daughter, all pretty and interesting children. Ai Toder is a very nice place, and they spend a great deal of time in the Crimea.

In walking through Yalta one hears so many different tongues, and sees so many nationalities that I was reminded of the day of Pentecost in Jerusalem.

Here you meet a Turkish family, the women all closely veiled with the exception of one eye with which they closely scrutinise you. It makes you uncomfortable to see the one eye gazing at you and not to see anything in return. Again you will meet Tartars-lively looking people, tall, and generally slight and athletic looking. They would need to be athletic, as they generally perch their villages on the top of an almost inaccessible cliff. They all dye their hair a vivid red, and the married women blacken their teeth and paint the palms of their hands. They say the Tartar houses are most beautifully clean.

The unmarried Tartar women only dye the hair; they wear on their heads a little round velvet cap with a veil hanging behind. This veil is of a sort of canvas, and is embroidered with gold and silver.

There are many Greeks who seem to do nothing but sleep in the Sull. They manage to live, however, and are, I believe, very shrewd in business. They seem contented with things in general though they are both ragged and dirty. Armenians, Greeks, full-blooded Russians, all in native costumes, make up a very pretty scene.

In Odessa and the Crimea the Karaites are principally found. These are a race of Tartars who embraced Judaism. They are a small tribe, only about ten thousand in all Russia. They are very good citizens, quite the best among the alien races in Russia. Their Judaism is of the Old Testament, and they entirely reject the Talmud, but to Western minds their ideas are peculiar and very wrong. Their women are taught no religion and can only hope to be saved through the intervention of their husbands; consequently their girls are married very young.

They are physically superior to the Jews, but they do not seem to increase rapidly. I met a Karaite family; well educated, nicely mannered people they were, some of them very handsome. They speak, even in their own houses, Russian, not the Tartar language, and are considered in every respect, except religion, as Russians.

It was while we were in the Crimea that the Emperor had typhoid fever. It was raging all round us at the time. At Ai Toder there were sixteen or seventeen cases. It was very bad in various Tartar villages higher up the mountains.

Those five weeks while he was lying ill were a very anxious time for the household, and great were the rejoicings when he recovered.

A little friend of the children, Paul, was ill at the same time with pneumonia. The doctors said recovery was doubtful. The Empress told me to call round there with the children in the carriage, and take poor little Paul a few roses and anything likely to tempt his appetite. Accordingly we got a few roses, packed a basket with delicacies, and went to inquire. The whole household was in despair; they had had a visit from a specialist that day, and his verdict had been unfavourable. We saw the children's English governess and she gave me a very sad account of poor little Paul. She took up the roses and basket, and told him the Imperial children had brought them to him, and were down in the garden waiting to know how he was. Paul sent his thanks to the children, and then said, "Send Daria to me." The little sister was accordingly sent for and came into the room in a very subdued and meek manner to receive Paul's parting charges. "Daria," said the supposed dying child, "you see the Imperial children think a great deal more of me than they do of you; when you had a cold they did not even send to inquire by telephone. They have come themselves, and have brought me all these good things. I am going to eat them and get well." Comforted with this thought he fell asleep and eventually did get well.

Chapter XV: The Little Prison Opener

WE spent Christmas that year in the Crimea, and brought in quantities of holly and ivy to decorate the house. Holly does not grow in the north of Russia at all; the climate is too severe for it.

The children were greatly charmed with the decorations, and pulled each other under the mistletoe for kissing purposes. A heavy fall of snow had blocked up the railway lines, and we were afraid there would be no Christmas parcels from either England or Gatchina. However, the special messengers had taken sledges and come across the mountains, so the gifts were all received on Christmas Eve in time for the trees. We had our Christmas tree as usual, and little Marie was specially delighted with it, as she could not remember anything of the kind. She said to the Emperor, who was just beginning to get about, "Papa, did you ever see anything so beautiful?"

It was late in January when we left the Crimea. We were all in bed on board the Standart when a special messenger came on board bringing the news of the death of Queen Victoria. The telegram was not opened till next morning; the Empress was greatly grieved. There was much searching for mourning, and fortunately everyone had something black with them.

We arrived in St. Petersburg on Saturday, and I had a rush to get a suitable hat to wear at church on Sunday. The church was crowded and everyone there was dressed in mourning, some even wore crepe. I never saw anything so melancholy in my life.

There were, of course, no balls given that year on account of the heavy mourning. The Crown Prince of Austria came on a visit. He had a quiet time, but some dinners were given in his honour. On one occasion there was a large dinner party in the Winter Palace. The Major Domo carried in a dish of fish, and began to hand it round; suddenly he fell - the fish was spilt on the carpet and the Empress's dress. In great confusion he got out of the room; he then came in with another dish; some of the fish must have remained on the carpet for the unfortunate man again fell and gave the Empress a liberal helping of whatever he was carrying. The second time was too much. All the company simply laughed till they were tired.

Though there was no ball season, the children began to go out a great deal, and to give little parties at home.

One day the little Grand Duchess Marie was looking out of the window at a regiment of soldiers marching past, and exclaimed, "Oh! I love these dear soldiers; I should like to kiss them all!" I said, "Marie, nice little girls don't kiss soldiers." She made no remark. A few days afterwards we had a children's party, and the Grand Duke Constantine's children were amongst the guests. One of them, having reached twelve years of age, had been put into the Corps de Cadets, and came in his uniform. He wanted to kiss his little cousin Marie, but she put her hand over her mouth and drew back from the proffered embrace. "Go away, soldier," said she, with great dignity. "I don't kiss soldiers." The boy was greatly delighted at being taken for a real soldier, and not a little amused at the same time.

I saw a great deal of St. Petersburg that year, and visited, amongst other places of interest, the Mint. I believe it is the largest in the world. When I went they were minting gold. They do all the melting with wood fires, great furnaces. I do not know how the men can stand over them. They have a piece of gold there which the Grand Duke Vladimir himself refined. In comparison to it an English sovereign looks like copper. One of the workmen invented a table by which gold can be counted very quickly. This table is all divided into little squares; one thousand ten-rouble pieces exactly fills each square. They can count them about twenty thousand pieces of money in an incredibly short space of time. Some of the machinery used is of a very fine and delicate nature. They mint here for the whole Russian Empire, and here, too, are struck the medals and decorations in use in Russia.

I also saw the cathedral of Notre Dame de Kazan. There are always many worshippers in the Russian churches. One poor woman was walking down the church on her knees. In the church itself were sellers of holy pictures. A lady who was with me suggested she would buy me one of these and I should buy her one in memory of this visit. I agreed, and she accordingly chose for herself the Madonna and Child. I paid for it forty kopecks, which is about ten pence of our money. This included in the blessing, so it was cheap enough. It was now my turn to choose, and I liked one with a picture of St. George and the Dragon. It struck me as being such a beautiful thing for adoration. I put it up in my sitting-room across one of the corners. Later on, the old archbishop, who gave the little Grand Duchess Olga religious instruction, came to lunch with me. He looked at this icon, and said, "But your name is not Georgette, is it?" I answered, "No, father; but it was given to me by a friend." "Oh!" said he, "and his name was George!" and he nodded his head in a most knowing way. It so happens that my friend is called Lilian. But I let it pass.

We also visited the cathedral of St. Isaac. This, of course, is not the Isaac of the Bible but a more modern saint. With the exception of Westminster Abbey, I know of no church which pleases more than St. Isaac. There is a beautiful golden screen, and pillars of malachite, lapis lazulias and Italian marble. I particularly admired the bronze doors; the workmanship of them is very beautiful. Personally, I seldom admire icons; they are curious, but not to my mind beautiful; but St. Isaac's contains some very fine specimens. I stood under the dome, and, looking up, saw a dove apparently life-size. I was afterwards told it measured twelve feet from the tip of one wing to the tip of the other.

The nursery party went to Tsarskoe Selo very early that year, the Emperor and Empress staying on in St. Petersburg. We returned to town at Easter, going back to Tsarskoe Selo until it was time to go to Peterhoff. Just before we went to Peterhoff that year, the Grand Duchess Olga had typhoid fever. She had been ailing for a few days, but the weather was unusually hot for the time of the year, and we thought that might be the cause and that the cooler air of the seaside would probably be beneficial to her, so the journey was not postponed. But when we arrived at Peterhoff she was very ill, and had to be put to bed at once. She lay there through five long weary weeks. I nursed her day and night, and at one time she was so ill that I feared she would not recover; but thank God she did. She wearied to see her sister Tatiana, and was very pleased when the doctor said Tatiana might pay her a visit for just five minutes. I went down and fetched her to see Olga. She stood by the side of the bed and conversed in a most amiable manner to the little sick sister. I was rather surprised at her manner, and when the five minutes were up, told her I must take her down to the nursery again. When she got outside of the door, she exclaimed: "You told me you were bringing me to see Olga and I have not seen her." I told her that the little girl in bed was indeed her sister. She cried with great grief. "That little pale thin child is my dear sister Olga! Oh no, no! I cannot believe it!" She wept bitterly at the change, and it was difficult to persuade her that Olga would soon be herself again.

Olga was still in bed when little Anastasie was born. Anastasie means "the breaker of chains," or "the prison opener," and in the icon sacred to her she is always represented with broken fetters behind her. The little Grand Duchess was called by this name because, in honour of her birth, the Emperor pardoned and reinstated the students who had been imprisoned for participating in the riots in St. Petersburg and Moscow during the winter. Alas! many of them were soon after in a state of revolution.

I cannot tell why the students are so restless in the Russian universities. They must know that in no country is the Government committed into the hands of young men studying for their professions. We are told that there is little or no entrance examination, no age disqualifications, and the fees are very low. Every professor has a certain number of free students who are elected to the order in which they apply. Many of these students have been failures, more or less, in other branches of life, and naturally enough they are also failures in the universities. When they fail in their examinations they say the examiners favoured so-and-so because he is rich, quite regardless of the fact that failure to pass an examination does not affect these free scholarships at all.

The anarchists, of whom many are to be found in the universities in the guise of students, find these discontented men an easy prey, but tell them they will always be passed over in life till all men are equal, etc. Sipiaguin and Plevhe were both murdered by students.

Sipiaguin's murderer was hanged, because for the purpose of getting near his victim he assumed the uniform of an officer, and represented that he was aide-de-camp to the Grand Duke Serge, who had sent him with a letter to the university; he refused to give any account of himself, and was consequently tried as an officer by the War Council, who alone can pass sentence of death in Russia. There is no capital punishment except for military offences.

All university students wear uniform. The constitution of the Russian universities may be the cause of the frequent outbreaks among the students. It is sad to think of the mischief done to the cause of education and to the more serious students, and the great loss of time and enforced idleness, when, as so often happens, the universities are closed for three or even six months.

Recently the students organised a meeting of protest against something or other, and held it in the Nevsky, the principal street in St. Petersburg. They chose the front of the cathedral of St. Kazan to make their speeches. Divine service was going on at the time, and naturally enough the police ordered them to clear. They refused to do so, so the Cossacks charged them, using their whips pretty freely. One woman student threw a smoothing iron and killed a young Cossack officer on the spot. This enraged the Cossacks, who pressed the students more closely. The latter took refuge in the church; stones were thrown and the officiating priest was struck on the head and severely wounded. Some hundreds of students, including many women, were arrested. They protested that they had only come out to walk just to amuse themselves, and were hemmed in by the Cossacks, and were only fighting to get clear of the crowd.

The authorities thought it was best to send them to the country for a while, and the ringleaders were put in prison.

The Grand Duchess Anastasie Nicolaivna was baptised when she was a fortnight old. I was not present at the ceremony as the Grand Duchess Olga had not yet quite recovered from the fever. But the ceremony was exactly the same at that observed for the baptism of the Grand Duchess Marie.

Many people have expressed surprise that one of the little Grand Duchesses was not called Victoria or Alexandra. The Russian Church only allows names which exist in the language. Victoria does not exist, though Victor does; Alexandra is considered very unlucky for the Romanoff family.

The Emperor Paul had a daughter named Alexandra. Her life was short, but troubled. When she was about seventeen years of age her grandmother, Catherine II, arranged a marriage for her with the King of Sweden. The wedding-day arrived, the bride was dressed, the tables laid for the feast, the guests assembled and the priests in waiting. The bridegroom suddenly declared to his gentlemen that he could not and would not go on with the marriage. Vainly they implored him not to insult his chosen bride and the great Russian nation. He was obstinate.

The bride and her family waited for him. Presently a very frightened and trembling courtier crept timidly into the room, and throwing himself on the ground before the august Catherine, broke the terrible news to her. She was already angry at the delay and her wrath was terrible to witness.

The King of Sweden and his suite left the Winter Palace as quickly as possible. A marriage was speedily arranged for the poor humiliated young Grand Duchess with an Austrian Grand Duke, but she never recovered the shock, and died broken-hearted at nineteen years of age.

Nicholas I had a very beautiful daughter named Alexandra. She was married to the step-son of Napoleon Bonaparte. She died of scarlatina before she was twenty years of age. There is a beautiful statue to her memory at Tsarskoe Selo, also a lovely little memorial church.

Alexandra II. had a daughter of the name; she died in childhood; a pretty golden-haired child she was, judging by her portrait. A little blue silk frock which she used to wear is still shown in the Winter Palace.

Other branches of the family had also Alexandras, but in no case did they live to be twenty-one years of age.

Chapter XVI: My First Meeting with the King

WE went to Denmark that year. There was a great gathering of Royalties there, including the King and Queen of England, Princess Victoria of England, and her sister, Princess Charles of Denmark, the Emperor and two Empresses of Russia, the King of Greece with one of his sons, and many other Royalties.

We stayed at Fredenburg that time. It is a good way from Copenhagen, and is a great deal bigger than Bernstorff. There is a large park there.

King Edward VII arrived after we did, and the day he was expected Queen Alexandra came into the nurseries and told me he was coming, and asked me to make the children look very nice. I showed her the dresses I had prepared for them, and she admired them very much. She often said they were always so nicely dressed and kept. When we were leaving the Queen gave me a photograph (signed) of herself, the King and his little grand-children, with such kind and gracious words as she only can speak.

The King frequently spoke to me, too, and called me "My Irish subject." He has very winning manners and great tact. He has a marvellous memory. This year he sent me, in memory of the birth of the Czarovitch, a brooch, in green enamel, because I am Irish. They say he never forgets anything, and I know he never forgets to be kind.

We saw a good deal of the Empress's family that year, as her eldest sister, Princess Louis of Battenberg, her husband, and all her family stayed with us in Peterhoff during the summer.

Princess Louis of Battenberg has four beautiful children. I think her two daughters are about the handsomest of the young grown-up princesses of Europe. The eldest one, Princess Alice, was married to the Prince Andre of Greece last year; she is very pretty, but I admire the younger sister more. They were both charming young girls, and she has two fine boys.

Some years ago now Prince Louis's ship was stationed in the Shannon. He went over to Kilkee to spend one night and see the place. Quite close to the station is a hotel, very nice and comfortable, but not first-class.

The Prince took a room in the hotel, left his bag, and went for a stroll. He had observed that the room contained two beds. When he returned to the hotel he was surprised to find one bed occupied by a commercial traveller. He sent for the manageress, and asked for a room for himself. She was exceedingly angry and scolded him violently, winding up with, "I'd like to know who you are to object to anyone. I'm sure you are no better than a little commercial traveller yourself." The Prince replied that all that might be very true, still he would like a room to himself. Whereupon the woman told him he might have a room in a small cottage which she had taken outside the hotel. The Prince accordingly went to the little cottage and slept there.

Prince Louis signed his name in the visitors' book in the morning, and the woman's horror and consternation may better be imagined than described. She was absolutely sure that the Queen would have her arrested for having been impertinent to her son-in-law, as she called him.

I was in Kilkee at the time the incident occurred, but could hardly believe the story, but the Prince himself assured me that it was absolutely true, and was greatly amused at the idea of meeting anyone from that remote spot in the Imperial Palace of Peterhoff.

Chapter XVII: Lost in the Forest

BUT to return to Riel and our journey to Spala. As a general rule, when the hour for departure was late, the children and I went down to the train early in the evening when they were putting in the luggage, and we were then shunted into a siding, and I got the children to bed in good time quietly and comfortably and they slept till morning.

On this occasion there was no siding long enough to hold the train, so orders had been given that we were to move slowly up and down, and arrangements had been made that we should not disturb the general traffic.

We were hardly in the train when it went off at a perfectly terrific rate-eighty-five miles an hour I was afterwards told. In a few minutes we were all desperately sick from the rocking. The poor children were terrified. I feared every moment the train would topple over. The servants were on their knees praying; everyone was upset.

With great difficulty I made my way to the engineer to beg him to reduce the speed. He was very sorry, said he had not had any idea that the results of going at such a pace would be so frightful, but he could not now reduce the speed, as the risk of running into other traffic was too great. Our train was too long and heavy, and he could not stop it now, not even for five minutes. He wished to try the engines, he said, and thought that a good opportunity. For nearly four hours we rushed up and down in the darkness, through Germany, at this rate. Fortunately I had got the children to bed, and they slept, poor little mites, worn out by the fright and crying.

Both my elbows were bruised and sore, and my face suffered, too, from being dashed against the furniture and falling on the floor. The Emperor and Empress were greatly shocked at our appearance, and the Emperor was really angry when he heard what had happened. I felt sick and giddy for a week after; it was more trying than a sea voyage.

The Empress had given me a present of a nice dressing-bag. I had it with me in the wagon, and saw it put out on the station at Spala; it, however, never arrived at the house. It was stolen probably by one of the carters, and though we offered rewards we never heard of it. The priest even spoke from the altar, and said if it was only returned no questions would be asked, but it was never found. I was very sorry, as I had many little things in it which I valued exceedingly, and also a diary which I had kept concerning the children. The police even instituted a search in the neighbouring town, but all of no avail. I have already spoken of the forest in Spala, and while we were there a little child born the same day as the Grand Duchess Marie, and therefore about two years and four months old, was lost in this forest. She was the youngest child of one of the keepers, and was playing near her mother while the latter was preparing dinner. The door was open, and the wee thing toddled out and wandered away. The mother thought she was playing in the little garden, and was quite easy about her.

When the father came home to dinner the baby could not be found. Soon every man about the place was hunting for the lost child. The Emperor stayed at home from shooting that day, and guards, police, keepers, foresters and others all turned out to seek for the lost child. The terrible fear was that she had been carried off by some wild beast.

A cordon was drawn round twenty miles of the forest, and searched carefully. Neighbours stayed with the poor distracted mother, and a fire was kept up and hot water and soup, etc., were always ready. To add to the distress heavy snow fell. All night and far into the next afternoon search was continued, but without result, till a soldier who had been out all night and was returning saw something fluttering under a bush. Drawing near he found the little one on her hands and knees under the bush, soaked through and perfectly unconscious. He quickly carried her home; she was undressed and put to bed, and given restoratives. In the evening she was quite recovered playing about the cottage home, and she very speedily forgot the whole story. It was a good thing she was so young, or the effect on her mind might have been disastrous.

We used to go on long drives about Spala in a little pony carriage with just the coachman. I began to be afraid that it was not quite safe as an accident might happen to the ponies, and none of us spoke one word of Polish, and it would have been impossible to send for help if anything did occur, so I asked that a Cossack might be sent after us on horseback.

This was accordingly done. The first day after the change was made we were driving through a village when we saw a man running down a hilly field towards us. He was clad only in his night-shirt. I thought he must have escaped from his bed, in delirium, and that he might be suffering from smallpox or typhoid, so was rather frightened. However, as soon as he saw the Cossack he turned and ran in another direction without attacking us in any way.

Next day he was found, in the same costume, in a wood at some distance from the village. The police asked him who he was. He professed to be amazed at their ignorance, and proclaimed himself as the King of Poland. One of the police asked him, "Where is your passport?" "What!" he said; "you are a policeman, and don't know that a king has no need of a passport." He proved to be a dangerous lunatic much addicted to stone throwing.

When we stayed in Poland we generally took a certain number of local people into the house as servants, not that we wanted them, but just to give them employment.

I never saw such dirty people; they ran about the house in bare feet, often covered with mud from the roads. Their costumes consisted of a striped woollen petticoat, a black cloth three-quarter length jacket, a striped woollen apron tied over it, a similar apron round their heads or tied by the strings round the shoulders like a kind of shawl. They would only speak Polish, and professed not to understand when addressed in Russian, though I afterwards found, when it came to a question of getting money, that they not only understood perfectly all that was said, but could read and write Russian with very few exceptions. The Russian who was paying them laughed heartily at my amazement at hearing them answer him in Russian and sign their names in the book for the money they received, but a golden key is very powerful all the world over.

Some time ago in St. Petersburg a lady whom I knew very slightly met me and said, "I gave that person you sent me twelve roubles, but I think it only right to tell you that I fear she is an impostor." Greatly amazed I asked her what she meant.

She told me a lady had called to see her; said she was a Pole and a great friend of mine and knew me intimately in Tsarskoe Selo; that I had helped her as much as I could, and then evidently sent her amongst my friends and acquaintances to levy contributions on them. Miss C. offered her five roubles (about ten shillings), but she said it would be useless to her; she must have twelve to pay her rent, or she and her five children would be turned out in the snowy streets. Had her case not been urgent I would not have sent her, and so forth. Needless to say I knew absolutely nothing of the woman.

A couple of days after this she visited the Winter Palace, but not me; she knew better than that. She visited Madame G. and asked her to give her a situation in any capacity in the nurseries under me. Vainly Madame G. assured her there was no vacancy. "We could easily make one," she declared. She then begged for ten roubles and refused to stir till one of the Polish ministers was called upon. He sent for her to his room, and her story of her five little children was so sad that he gave her twenty roubles, and promised to make inquiries and get her work.

She was not known at the address given.

She next was heard of at the Grand Duchess Olga Alexandrovna's house, and went away with money and a good deal of work. The Grand Duchess was greatly interested in her.

She turned up at the Grand Duke Serge's house in Moscow, when she said she was Madame G., and had been called suddenly to the south of Russia, and was about thirty roubles short for her journey. Would Mademoiselle D. lend it to her, or should she apply to the Governor?

It so happened that a personal friend of Madame G. was present, and was delighted at the prospect of seeing her, and went downstairs. To her amazement she was confronted by a stranger who explained that she was Madame G.'s servant.

Her mother was very ill in the south, and she had got a telegram saying to go at once if she wished to see her alive. Madame G. had hurried her off, but had not sufficient money to pay for the journey; she had told her to call at the Governor's house and mademoiselle would give her the money.

She had been in Madame G.'s employment for ten years, knew all about her rooms, and spoke so fluently that this money was given. Needless to say, no one belonging to any of the palaces ever saw either the woman or the money again.

Chapter XVIII: Concerning the Children

WE returned to Tsarskoe Selo early in November, and stayed there till after Christmas, then as usual went to St. Petersburg for New Year's Day.

There was a very gay season that year, many bails and dinners and supper parties. The year before there was no gaiety owing to the Court being in mourning for Queen Victoria.

The Crown Prince of Germany paid us a visit, and became very intimate with his little cousins. His visit was spoiled, however, by an attack of influenza.

The early part of the year passed just as usual. The little Grand Duchess Tatiana now began to learn English reading and writing; Olga's education was of course much further advanced. She had masters for music and Russian. Both children have a very marked talent for music; the Empress and some of her sisters are very musical, but the Emperor neither plays nor sings. He is, however, very fond of music. He told me he could not learn because his masters insisted on his playing by note, and he preferred picking up tunes he liked by ear.

One day the arithmetic master, a professor of algebra from one of the universities, wished Olga to write something; she asked his leave to go in to the Russian master, who was teaching little Tatiana in the next room. He said she could go, but asked her what she wanted to say to him. She told him she could not spell "arithmetic." He told her how this difficult word was written, and she exclaimed, with great admiration, "How clever you are! and how hard you must have studied to be able, not only to count so well, but to spell such very long words!" She thought me a marvel of education, and confided in her music master that no one in the whole world knew so much as I did; she thought I knew everything, except music and Russian.

Though she is in some things advanced beyond most children of her age, in others she is far behind them. This arises, of course, from her very sheltered life.

On one occasion the milliner brought them new hats, with which she was greatly pleased; she told me she thought Madame B. was the very kindest woman in the world. "She went all the way to Paris," she said, "and brought us a present of those beautiful hats." I explained that it was Madame's business, and that the hats had been bought, not given as a present. She looked a little puzzled, and then said, "I am afraid you are making a mistake; you did not give her any money, and I know she did not go to mama for it."

Her only knowledge of shops and shopping was derived from the toy and sweet shops in Darmstadt. One day she asked me why the Americans spoke English, not American. I told her the story of the Pilgrim Fathers, and described how they built houses and shops, and so made towns. She was exceedingly interested and inquired, "Where did they find the toys to sell in the shops?"

I was reading "Alice in Wonderland" and "Through the Looking-Glass" to them lately, and she was horrified at the manners of the queens. "No queens," she said, "would be so rude." When I read about Alice's journey by railway she was exceedingly amused, and thought it very funny that she had not a compartment to herself. I told her in travelling each person took one ticket and occupied just one seat in the train, and told her some tickets cost more than others, and the highest-priced tickets meant a better place in the train.

She listened and said, "And when you travel can anyone with the same kind of ticket you have get into the same carriage as you do? "I told her, "Yes." So she said, "If I were you, I should take a whole compartment for myself." I said, "But you forget that these other people might object to me, and say, 'I won't sit beside that person.'"

"Oh no," said she. "Everyone in the whole world would be glad to sit beside you."

Lately she was reading some little stories from English history; she read about the English cutting off the Welsh Prince Llewellyn's head, and sending it to London. She was awfully shocked, and read the story again. Then she exclaimed, "Well, it was a good thing he was dead before they cut off his head; it would have hurt him most awfully if he was alive." I said that they were not always so kind, and sometimes cut the heads off living people, and later she would read of them doing such things. She said, "Well, I really think people are much better now than they used to be. I'm very glad I live now when people are so kind."

Chapter XIX: Chersonese

ON our way to the Crimea in the autumn of 1902 we passed the spot where the Imperial train was wrecked some sixteen or seventeen years ago.

A church has been erected, and the Emperor and Empress, with the little Grand Duchess Olga, attended divine service there. Many curious stories of hair-breadth escapes from death have been told me concerning this accident.

Electricity was used for the first time in the Imperial train on this journey. The train got most uncomfortably hot, and the Empress thought there was something wrong with the electrical engines, so she sent for the engineer and asked him to see why the train was so hot.

Taking his assistant with him he went into the engine-room; it was very hot there, and both men soon laid aside their coats and worked in their shirt-sleeves.

It was still too hot, and in spite of the remonstrance of his assistant, the engineer opened the window. In another moment the first shock of the explosion, or whatever wrecked the train was felt, and the two men were sent flying out of the window and down the slope. They fell about thirty feet, and arrived unhurt in the snow.

But many were killed and wounded; in one compartment two officers had put their swords in the netting over their heads. The swords fell out of the sheathes and struck them on the backs of their heads, killing them outright. The Secretary was precipitated through the window, and falling on his head, turned over and broke his neck.

The Imperial family were at luncheon when it occurred. The servant was just handing a dish of calves' brains to the Emperor when suddenly the shock threw them all to the ground. Most of them, including the present Emperor, found themselves under the table.

The Emperor was the first to recover; he was shocked to see the servant lying apparently dead, his face covered with blood and brains, and exclaimed with horror, "Oh! Poor fellow! His brains are dashed out."

The supposed corpse sat up and began to speak; he had cut his head in the fall and the brains were not his, but those of the calf.

The little Grand Duchess Olga Alexandrovna was thrown, with her nurse, through the window. They were both cut and bruised and the nurse sustained internal injuries, but nothing very serious; it was a wonderful escape. In all, about thirty people lost their lives, but none of the Imperial family were seriously injured.

Some say it was the work of anarchists. If so, they selected their spot with a care and ingenuity worthy of a better cause, as just in that place the ground dips and falls about thirty feet downwards from the railway. For miles on each side the track is perfectly level.

Others say that the lines had spread and so the train was turned over. Less than an hour before the pilot train, carrying most of the suite, had passed over in perfect safety.

We lay at anchor several days in Sevastopol harbour, and made several excursions to the town and adjacent country.

A battleship for the Black Sea Squadron was launched while we were there. Every night the harbour and fleet were illuminated and looked most beautiful. The children were delighted with the appearance of the ships and greatly puzzled as to how it was done.

However, we got to Sevastopol safely. The town is situated on high cliffs, and looks inaccessible from the water side; it is very open at the rear. The town still bears marks of the siege. It is all paved with cobble stones and is the noisiest place in the world for its area, I feel sure. It is picturesque. We were there early in October and the heat was intolerable. No rain falls during the summer months, and everything looks dried and choked with dust.

We passed through the famous quarries - where the English lay entrenched and so much desperate fighting took place. Beyond these quarries are the graveyards where lie the victims, or some of them, of the war.

To understand something of the horrors of war we should visit, in cold blood the battle-fields, and see the graves of the fallen, and then count up as far as possible profits and losses. I feel sure that the vote would be given against the waste of human lives.

We visited the English graveyard. The piece of ground was bought from Russia and is enclosed with a stone wall, the entrance is handsome, and the whole place is kept in beautiful order. There is a resident caretaker, a Russian, who keeps all trim, and plants and tends flowers and shrubs with great care. Parts of the walls are festooned with clematis and plumbago, which flourish exceedingly. In the spring the Judas tree is a mass of purple blossoms. Humbler flowers, such as snapdragon, scabius, cornflowers, etc., grow on the graves. But those graves! The inscriptions on them are sad beyond belief.

A black marble slab bore the name of a young woman, and underneath that of a three days old baby, evidently her son, but nothing more to tell whose daughter and wife she had been, nor under what circumstances she had come out to perish at twenty-one years of age with her infant son in a far land, amid the strain and stress of war.

One stone covers the remains of four youthful officers. The inscription sets out that though unrelated, and in different regiments, they were bound together by their youth, heroism, and love of country. They fell in one battle and were buried in one grave. Their ages were from seventeen to twenty-one years, united they would not have been eighty. Poor boys! Who can tell how many hopes and fears, ambition, and love lie buried with them.

In one grave lie the remains of over four hundred men who fell together. I found the grave of a hero of whom I had read much in my youthful days, Captain Headley Vicars. He lies with his head to the wall; his grave is well kept. He was only twenty-seven years of age. In so short a life we would have thought there was little room for distinction, but his name will long be remembered for his great piety. "He rests from his labours, and his works do follow him." He was killed in the quarries one night.

On the other side of Sevastopol lies Chersonese, the lately excavated city. It was founded in the fourth century and was burned in the fourteenth by a horde of warlike Tartars. Some years ago something was dug up on the property of a local gentleman which led him to believe that the buried city lay under his property. Excavations were began and were crowned with victory. They found the remains of what was the chief street of the city. Portions of the houses remained and human remains lay about in all directions. They gathered these ghastly things and buried them. In many of the houses cooking operations had evidently been going on when sudden death overtook the inhabitants. There were many burned and charred loaves of bread taken from the ovens. There are also five eggs quite intact which were found in one of the houses. Fancy eggs more than five hundred years old!

There is a great deal of beautiful cut stone work; also various articles of pottery and glass. Many of the specimens look like old-fashioned silver lustre. Some of the articles are very graceful in shape.

There is also gold and silver jewellery set with precious stones and some precious stones, chains, brooches, and long, heavy ear-rings, also bracelets. Many of these were set with turquoise which had kept their colour wonderfully well.

The jawbone of a woman had each tooth filed to a point. The owner of it must have been a person of consideration in her own circles, for though they found hundreds of jawbones this was the only one with the teeth so decorated. Or perhaps she was the first to adopt a new fashion in teeth and the other ladies of Chersonese were waiting to see what their lords and masters thought of it before taking to it. I should suppose she would have suffered terribly from toothache. One thing that struck me about the jaw was its exceeding smallness.

In one of the houses papers were found containing, amongst other valuable information, a plan of the city, and of the church, which had been excavated just before our visit.

The church was surrounded by four wells, north, south, east, and west. The water in three of them was brackish and bitter, that in the fourth was sweet and good for drinking. There were catacombs underneath the church and the mosaic on the floor of the church was described at length.

A few days before we visited the place the fourth well had been discovered. The three others had been discovered some little time before, and all three contained brackish water, but the fourth was sweet and quite good for use. There was great excitement about it, but nothing on earth would induce me to drink it, nor to allow the children to do so; I am not fond of trying experiments, and should not like to drink water which had been shut up for five hundred years.

Some of our party went down to see the catacombs, and one of them kicked over a skull, but I preferred to remain in the sunlight of the upper world. They found quantities of human remains there. The stairs leading down to them are in good repair.

The walls of the church stand to about the height of four feet, and have been strongly cemented on the top to try to keep them together. In one end of the church there is built into the fabric a semi-circular seat where the priests used to sit; it would hold twelve comfortably, but the floor is in beautiful repair. The mosaics are most extraordinary; there are patterns of birds, chalices, crosses, etc., all linked into a harmonious whole and all executed with the common pebbles from the sea-shore. They were rubbed and polished by the feet and knees of dead and gone worshippers.

The church is cruciform in shape. Tradition says it was built by Vladimir, the first Christian ruler of Russia, to commemorate his baptism which took place in a little chapel which had been incorporated into a monastery built on the top of a hill at a little distance off.

In the Winter Palace is a picture of the heads of Vladimir, Peter the Great, and Alexander II, joined together in the one painting, because they gave the three great gifts of Christianity, civilisation, and freedom to their country.

The gentleman who had carried out these most interesting excavations came down to see the Imperial children, and showed them all the Museum. He afterwards congratulated me most earnestly; he said he had never seen such young children take so intelligent an interest in antiquities, and he was sure I must often have talked to them on such subjects, etc. Had he only known it was their good manners he also ought to have admired, as the poor little ones did not understand much of what they heard. For one thing they were too young, and for another, in deference to me, he spoke in French.

That year in the Crimea we saw a great deal of Princess Ellen, now of Servia. She was a very sweet-faced though plain girl, with beautiful dark eyes, very quiet and amiable in manner. The little Grand Duchess Olga was very fond of her, and Princess Ellen would often come to tea in the nurseries, her young aunt, Princess Vera of Montenegro, and the young cousins with whom she lived most of the time. Princess Ellen was about seventeen years of age. Her mother had been dead for many years and she lived chiefly with one or other of the aunts in Russia. What a change has come into her life! I often think of her with deep pity and compassion. She can never know an easy moment, surrounded as she is by the assassins of the late king and queen. Poor, gentle, amiable girl! What will be her fate?

The Shah of Persia sent his conjuror over to the Emperor that year, and he performed for the children, who gave a large party of their friends, including Princess Ellen, to see him. He was really a most wonderful performer and did many extraordinary tricks. We had placed all the little ones in the front row and when he produced a pair of live pigeons from a pudding their joy knew no bounds. He presently produced a guinea pig, passed his hand over it, and lo! There were two in his hands. In a moment three little girls were on the platform, and eager voices cried, "Oh! Please, Mr. Conjuror, make me a guinea-pig for myself." My three eldest charges attacked him with beseeching eyes and hands. I verily believe he would have given them his trained guinea pigs, but I ran and stopped him, telling the children that the little animals were so fond of their master, and would be unhappy if taken away, I managed to get them into the hall again.

The nights in the Crimea are usually dark, and the roads exceedingly bad, so when we went out to tea our carriage was always preceded by a common cart, in which were tar barrels and torches to light us. The roads, many of which went up frightful mountains, are most unsafe.

The season of 1903 was exceptionally brilliant; the great event was the famous costume ball which was given in the old part of the palace, and at the request of the various Embassies was repeated in the new part.

All present were arrayed in the costumes worn at the court of the Emperor Alexis, father of Peter the Great. The Empress went dressed as his first wife, and her ladies-in-waiting copied their dresses from pictures of costumes worn by the belles of his court. The Empress's dress was indeed magnificent. It was in cloth of gold embroidered in pearl beads. The whole front of it was encrusted with precious stones, and had ropes of pearls down the sides. She wore her emeralds with it, and had a crown made especially for the occasion, decorated with emeralds.

Her dress and jewels cost upwards of a million roubles, more than a hundred thousand pounds of our money. It was, however, tremendously heavy and hot. The married ladies all wore the hair covered with a cloth resembling an embroidered napkin; the unmarried showed their hair. A very busy man was the coiffeur who dressed the hair, adding to the ladies' own tresses, curls or plaits.

Men's dress must have been most gorgeous in those days. Count Benkendorff, the Mareshal de la Cour, wore white satin tunic and knee-breeches trimmed with ermine, surmounted by a black velvet cape with a fur collar, and a small black velvet hat bound with ermine. He looked very well and exceedingly dignified. A couple of men came as falconers in doublets and hose and wearing yellow top-boots very much turned up at the toes. They had falcons chained to their wrists. Not a few were in chain armour. It was the gayest scene I have ever seen. They danced old-fashioned Russian dances which tell by gestures a story of courtship. The lady first pretends not to see her humble adoring swain, coming round by degrees, till finally they dance together, and walk up and down the hall, hand in hand, he evidently very pleased of his victory over the coy maiden, and she looking very demure and modest.

Chapter XX: The Priest

WE passed the year much as usual, only going to Moscow for Easter. On our return to Tsarskoe Selo the Empress manifested symptoms of whooping cough. It speedily spread to the nurseries and the four children. The Russian nurse and I contracted it. I had told the children they were to be most careful not to cough on anyone, or that person might take the disease from them, and they were very obedient. One day the little Grand Duchess Anastasie was sitting in my lap, coughing and choking away, when the Grand Duchess Marie came to her and putting her face close up to her said, "Baby, darling, cough on me." Greatly amazed, I asked her what she meant, and the dear child said, "I am so sorry to see my dear little sister so ill, and I thought if I could take it from her she would be better." Was it not touching?

But all things come to an end, even whooping cough, and one day when we were all well I went up to town to do some shopping. I was talking to the proprietor when a priest came in. He asked for what he wanted and then turned to me and said, "I heard your voice when I came in, and am sure you are a compatriot of mine. You are Irish, are you not?"

I answered his question in the affirmative, and he said he knew, and asked my name and from what part I came. He himself came from the same part, and knew some of my family.

He told me that though he was an Irishman his work lay in Glasgow, in the poorest and worst part of that town, down by the docks. From time to time poor Poles came to live in his parish, and he was sometimes called up to administer the sacraments to them, but owing to their mutual inability to understand each other, he could do little for them.

Out of pity for them, thus cut off from all religious comfort, he had undertaken to travel to Poland, and try to get into communication with the priests there, to get them a supply of prayer-books, catechisms, and other religious books which might be a help and solace to them in a far country in times of distress.

When I returned I told the Empress of his care over his flock. She begged me to thank him in her name for his care of and love for her poor Polish subjects, should I ever see him again. I am sorry to say I omitted to ask him his address. The Empress's words might have encouraged him in his task.

Should he by any chance see these words I take the opportunity of giving him the Empress's message, and of telling him that I have so often thought of and prayed for him, that God would bless him in his work. He is a good man.

Chapter XXI: Princess Ella

THERE was a great family gathering in Darmstadt in September, 1903, to celebrate the marriage of the Princess Alice of Battenberg (a daughter of the Empress's sister) to Prince Andre of Greece (a nephew of Queen Alexandra).

They had been engaged for quite two years, but owing to the extreme youth of both the marriage was postponed. The four Hessian sisters were all in Darmstadt, and at a ball given in their honour all looked lovely. Amongst the other guests were the Queen of England, who is closely related to both bride and groom, and Princess Victoria.

We stayed in the new palace. It was built, I believe, for Princess Alice and is a nice, roomy, comfortable residence, with a pretty garden and grounds, situated in the town of Darmstadt. There are ponds in the garden covered with lotus blossoms; they are like pink water-lilies and the seed pods are very pretty and decorative. I have never seen them in England, but they ought to do well enough, I should think.

My children were delighted to see their cousin Ella once more. This dear child was then between eight and nine years old, and very like her beautiful mother in appearance. But the child's eyes had ever a look of fate in them. Looking at her I used to wonder what those wide grey-blue eyes saw, to bring such a look of sadness to the childish face.

There is a modern picture by Josephine Swaboda, a Hungarian artist, of a Madonna and Child, and the Virgin's eyes might have been painted from that child's, so full of pathos and future sorrow do they seem. In spite of this look of intense sadness in her eyes the little Princess herself was full of life and happiness. I never saw so sunny a nature; I never saw the child out of temper, nor cross, and should any little dispute arise amongst my four charges, she would settle it with perfect amiability and justice, making whoever was the most in the wrong give in, and reproving with great gentleness the others. Where Princess Ella was, no angry disputes could exist. She was so sweet and just that the other children always gave in to her arbitration. Looking back on her short life I often wonder why we did not see that she was quite too good for this world, her fit companions were the angels. She was a regular little mother, and was never so happy as with the "tiny cousin," as she called Anastasie.

It was a pretty sight to see her riding with the two eldest cousins in the riding-school; she mounted on a great white horse and her cousins on little ponies. She rode wonderfully well, and would take either of the little ones before her on the saddle, and give them a ride round the school.

The wedding for which we came took place in the two churches, the Lutheran and the Greek.

The bride wore crepe de chine over liberty satin, trimmed with the beautiful and now historic lace formerly belonging to her grandmother, Princess Alice. This lace was worn by each of the Hessian Princesses on their wedding-days. The Grand Duke lent it to his niece for the occasion.

My little girls and their cousins were all dressed in white Honiton lace frocks and looked very sweet.

The ceremonies were very long, that in the Russian Church lasting nearly two hours. The chief feature of it is the holding of the crown over the heads of bride and groom, and their being led three times round the church.

One of the little ones was terribly distressed at learning that cousin Alice would have to leave her mother and go to live with her husband. "I'll never marry," said the little maid. "I couldn't leave my dear mama." I told her that everyone who was married had to go to live with husband or wife, and that cousin Andre would now live with cousin Alice, but that both of them would see their parents pretty often. She began to wonder why people married, when it meant separation, and I said, "Very few people can stay always with their father and mother, many people are obliged to go away and live with strangers without being married at all."

She was surprised and wanted to know if I had ever known anyone who did. I told her of several people who had done so, whom she knew, myself amongst the number, and that we were perfectly happy.

She considered a little, and then with a beaming smile said, "But that was different, our mama called you." There was a mother in it, in any case, she thought.

After the wedding was over and the guests gone we went out to Wolfsgarten, and were very happy there during the fine autumn weather. The Empress bought bicycles for her three eldest children and they had grand rides with their cousin about the place. They hunted the woods for mushrooms, of which many varieties are found in Germany, and had various excursions.

While we were in Wolfsgarten a carriage accident which might have had serious results happened. The Empress and her sister had just returned from a drive and were preparing to alight when the horses suddenly took fright and bolted. They rushed round the sides of the narrow court yard and suddenly headed for the stables, the door of which was shut. The footman, an old servant, thinking that a smash was inevitable, threw himself from the box, hoping to catch the horses by the heads and bring them to a standstill. He however fell and got kicked in the face by one of the horses. His wounds were slight, and he was quite recovered in a few days.

The Grand Duke of Hesse saw the occurrence and rushed up in time to catch one of the horses by the bridle as they were heading into the shut-up stable. The Empress and her sister sat quite quietly in the carriage, and did not appear at all dismayed by the accident. The Grand Duke acted with great pluck and presence of mind.

The children were fortunately all in the little cottage at the moment, so were out of danger. But they witnessed the whole thing from the windows, and were terribly frightened.

Our pleasant days in Wolfsgarten drew to a close, and we went to Skernivitsi, in Poland, taking the Grand Duke of Hesse and his little daughter with us.

She always enjoyed life so much, and she ran and bicycled about the gloomy old park, took the lead in all the games and was like a sunbeam; yet all the time she was stricken with mortal illness, though none suspected it. I got some of the men to erect a swing and a giant's stride for the children, and a great surprise had been prepared for them in the shape of a little carriage drawn by a pair of tame deer, so their mornings were passed pleasantly. In the afternoon we drove.

Poland is a very ugly country, but the child was deeply interested in all that she saw. Like myself, she was horrified at seeing the people kneel in the road whenever the children's carriage approached. As for me, I never got used to it, nor ever overcame the feeling of horror mixed with pity that I experienced on seeing this done for the first time. The little Grand Duchess Olga, who is very sensitive, used to look at them with tears in her eyes and beg of me to tell them not to do it.

The Russian Government had established many schools in Poland, and the younger generation is growing up with better ideas on such subjects.

The holy pictures hung upon the trees, the little shrines at the cross roads, the straw signs showing that men and horses could find accommodation, and the poor, dirty people themselves, all interested the little Hessian Princess to a wonderful extent.

One day she and Tatiana were wonderfully busy and mysterious, running in and out of the rooms, and exploding into laughter every now and then. In the evening after they were in bed Tatiana took from under her pillow a little box which dear cousin Ella had prepared for her. This contained some little coloured stones which they had picked out of the gravel the day before, some bits of matches, luminous ends, of course, the sand-paper off a match-box and some tissue paper. This was a toy which they had prepared. After Tatiana was in bed, if she felt lonely she was to sit up in bed, light a match upon the sand-paper, set fire to the tissue paper, and by its light to play with the stones. Well, of course, that could not be allowed, and the poor little Princess was overwhelmed when I explained to her that they might all have been burned in their beds.

One evening when the game was laid out, Miss W., Princess Ella's English nurse, said to me, "I should so much like to show my baby this, it would interest her." We got blankets and shawls and prepared a warm little nest for her in the window seat, and brought her from her bed, wrapped in a dressing-gown and shawl, to see the wonderful sight. She was quite delighted, and everyone came to the window and talked to her through it for a minute. Next morning the Grand Duchess Olga was disposed to grumble at having been left in bed all night, and said to me, "Ella is only eight months older than I am, and Miss W. took her up to see it all, and you left me in bed, like a baby." The little Princess said so sweetly, "Oh! dear Olga, don't be angry, you will often see it again, but I shall never again see it." She so often made use of this expression, "I shall never see it again," that I sometimes wonder if she had any premonition of approaching fate.

95

The shooting party went to Spala. The whole game shot during the two days was brought home earlier than usual on Saturday afternoon, and was all laid out before the children's bedtime, so Miss W. and I thought we might indulge our little charges with a sight of it all. We accordingly wrapped them up, and took them out and they were delighted. The little Princess was full of life and fun. I never remember to have seen her in higher spirits than she was on Saturday evening. She prepared and carried out an innocent little practical joke on her father and the Empress. She asked me to put her three eldest cousins in her bed, and leave little Anastasie alone in her bedroom. "When auntie Alix and papa come," said the child, "auntie Alix will be looking everywhere for her children, and papa will not know how he has got four." Accordingly it was done, and I stepped into the corridor to ask the Empress and the Grand Duke to be very much surprised. They were, of course, exceedingly surprised, and the Empress pretended to be much frightened, to the child's great delight. You could hear her laughter all through the house, as one by one the cousins were disclosed.

On Sunday morning Miss W. called out to me that her little one had a sore throat. It was then about half-past seven and she had just awakened. I immediately sent off for the court doctor, and we took her temperature, which was normal, so we thought she might be dressed. She had only began to make her toilette when other symptoms set in, and so she was put to bed again. The doctor came, but the throat was then better. He said it was possible that the change of food might have disagreed with her, but he was not in the least alarmed, and neither were we. I kept my little ones out as much as possible, to keep the nurseries quiet for the ailing little one. At four o'clock I returned from the drive with my little charges. Miss W. looked up quickly and said cheerfully, "Oh! my baby is ever so much better, she has had no return of the sickness for a couple of Hours, and is sleeping quietly." She then went into the room to the sick child.

I went to the doctor and congratulated him on the improvement in his little patient. "Improvement," he echoed, "the child is dying of failure of the heart." I felt stunned for a moment, then utterly incredulous, and reminded him that the child had been ill for hours, and that children run down quickly and recover quite as rapidly. He adhered to his statement that the child's heart was failing from hour to hour.

I had to tell the Empress and Grand Duke that the child was very ill and weak, and her temperature had risen rapidly till it was 104¼ Fahrenheit. They both came down to see her. Neither of them could see that she was very ill, nor in any danger. The doctor said the danger was from the heart, the beatings of it were hardly perceptible. The Grand Duke felt her pulse and thought it strong enough. They were in and out all through the evening and always thought the doctor and I were needlessly alarmed. So absolutely did they disbelieve in the possibility of any danger to the child that they went to the theatre that night.

After they had gone the doctor exclaimed that he would like a second opinion. I got him to send a message to the Empress, asking if we might send to Warsaw for some one. She sent back word to send a telegram and a special train for the best advice which could be got, but added that she and the child's father were both perfectly easy and happy about her. We accordingly sent off for a specialist. Before he came the Imperial family returned from the theatre. The Empress and the Grand Duke came in to see the little one, who roused herself and spoke brightly to them. The Empress told me not to be nervous or frightened about the child, that she would be all right in the morning. They went to bed, and the child speedily sank into a semi-stupor. I told Miss Wilson I could not leave her alone with her sufferer but would stay all night with her.

Presently the two little Grand Duchesses, Marie and Anastasie, began to scream, and I ran into their room; I found them both standing in their beds looking terribly alarmed. They told me there was a strange man in their room who had frightened them. Now the rooms were in a suite, and they could be entered only from the dining-room, or from the second bedroom, and this bedroom in its turn could only be entered from the room in which the little Princess lay ill. It will therefore be seen that no one could have entered their room without our knowledge. The doctor and the little Princess's own faithful servant-man had been in the dining-room all night. I thought the night-light might have thrown a shadow which frightened the children into thinking there was someone in the room. I therefore changed its position, but still the children were afraid, and said he was hiding over by the curtain. I lit a candle, and taking little Anastasie in my arms, carried her round the room to prove to her that there was absolutely nothing to frighten her. The doctor came in and tried to soothe Marie, but it was useless; she would not be soothed and

Anastasie refused to return to bed, so I took her in my arms and sat down to try to comfort her. She buried her face in my neck and clung to me trembling and shaking. It was dreadful to me to see her in such a fright. The doctor being obliged to go I lighted a candle and left it on a little table close to Marie's bed, and sat down near it, that I might be beside both children. Marie kept talking about the dreadful person, and starting up in wild horror every now and then. The doctor came in and out, and told me the strange doctor had come and had given the little sufferer an injection of caffeine; her heart seemed stronger and he began to have hope.

When next Marie began to talk about the mysterious stranger I said, "A strange doctor had come to help Dr. H. to make cousin Ella quite well, and perhaps he might have come to the door in mistake, or you might have heard him speak, but there is no one in the room now."

She assured me that the stranger was not a doctor and had not come through that door at all, and did not speak. Suddenly she stood up and looked at something which I could not see. "Oh!" she said, "he is gone into cousin Ella's room." Anastasie sat up on my knee and said, "Oh! poor cousin Ella; poor Princess Elizabeth!"

She fell asleep almost immediately after, but it was some time before I could loosen the clasped arms, and little Marie slept also quietly. As soon as possible I laid her in her little bed and returned to the sick room.

The strange doctor said to me when I entered the room, "The little child is no better." I asked him what was wrong, and he said, "Paralysis of the heart." He had given her many injections, both of caffeine and camphor, but to no avail.

We gave her stimulants constantly, and for a little she appeared to improve, and we hoped we might save her.

Suddenly she sat up in her bed, and looked from one to the other of us with wide, frightened eyes. She cried out suddenly, "I'm dying! I'm dying!" Miss W. coaxed her to lie down again.

The child turned to me, and said anxiously, "Send a telegram to mama." I promised it should be done, and she added, "Immediately."

We sent upstairs and called the Grand Duke and the Empress, who came down without loss of time. The telegram was sent to Coburg to the mother. Alas! It was too late; when her answer was received the child had already passed away.

We continued to fan the feeble spark of life, but moment by moment it declined. She began to talk to her cousins, and seemed to imagine she was playing with them. She asked for little Anastasie, and I brought the wee thing into the room. The dying eyes rested on her for a moment, and Anastasie said, "Poor cousin Ella! Poor Princess Elizabeth!" I took the baby out of the room.

Miss W. was kneeling beside the bed. The dying child turned and kissed her; another minute and her race was accomplished; the bright young life was ended. There was an autopsy made on the body. A German, and two Polish doctors, with the court doctor, did what was necessary.

They found she had died of suppressed typhoid, was twelve days ill, but it never showed.

She had died in the children's rooms, and it was thought better to remove them, in order that the necessary fumigation and disinfecting should be carried out. So we left for Tsarskoe Selo that same evening. The Emperor and Empress intended to go to the funeral, but the Empress got cold in the child's room, and inflammation of the ear set in, so she lay in Skernivitsi for six weeks, and we were in Tsarskoe Selo. It was a sad and gloomy time, the Empress lying ill in Poland, the children and their household in Tsarskoe Selo. Even Christmas was overshadowed, as, though the Emperor and Empress had returned, the latter was laid up with influenza, and the festivities without her were shorn of half their brightness. The Empress was ill till towards the middle of January. My children talked much of cousin Ella and how God had taken her spirit, and they understood that later God would take her body also to heaven.

On Christmas morning when Olga awoke, she exclaimed at once, "Did God send for cousin Ella's body in the night?" I felt startled at such a question on Christmas morning, but answered, "Oh no, dear, not yet." She was greatly disappointed, and said, "I thought He would have sent for her to keep Christmas with Him."

One day Marie was looking at a picture of Nydia, the blind girl of Pompeii; she asked me why she was blind. I replied that God sometimes made people blind, but none knew why. So she said, "I know someone who knows." I said, "No, dear, I think not; no one knows." "Cousin Ella knows," came the answer; "she is in heaven, sitting down and talking to God, and He is telling her how He did it, and why."

Chapter XXII: The Outbreak of War

WE returned to St. Petersburg towards the end of January, and the Court season began. This year it was destined to be broken off by the sudden outbreak of war in the East.

As usual about six large balls had been arranged for, and some theatrical entertainments, but it was all over in a very short time.

In the nurseries we had a few children's parties, but nothing very much. Little Anastasie was delighted with the stir and bustle of city life and deeply interested in all she saw. The children developed a love for those little toy balloons which are sold in the streets. When they were very good I used to send out and get them one each. But Anastasie used sometimes to want me to stop the carriage and buy them from the men, and this, of course, could not be allowed. So I always said simply that I could not, without advancing any reason. She evidently thought force would have to be used to induce him to part with them, for one day she saw some little children walking on the Palace Quay, each one with a balloon. She drew my attention to them. "Look, look!" cried she; "little children with balloons; get out, take them from them and give them to me." I explained why that would not do, so she said, "Well, get out, and ask them nicely and politely, and perhaps they will give them to me."

After the war broke out the children, even little Anastasie, worked at frame knitting. They made scarves for the soldiers, and Olga and Tatiana crocheted caps indefatigably. The Empress started working parties, and had more than five thousand ladies working for her.

Some of the work done was very peculiar: one girl sewed the sleeves of a shirt she was given to make, into the collar band; another had a pair of surgical trousers to make, and gathering them along the top, put them into a twenty-inch waist-band. It was very funny, but at the same time I doubt whether the same class of girls in any other country would have done better, for all these people belonged to the Court circles.

A band of girls came to the Empress and petitioned her to send them out to the war to nurse the wounded. Their request was refused, but the Empress said to them, "If you really wish to help you can go into the hospitals in St. Petersburg and work there, leaving the trained nurses free to go to the front." Without exceptions they all went and did what she suggested, and most of them stuck to it also. One girl, the belle of St. Petersburg, aged nineteen, got on so well that she was soon placed in charge of a ward for night-work.

One evening on coming to the hospital she found a young woman of the peasant class in charge of her work. She went to see the matron, who said, "I had a vacancy which I intended for my niece. You took it, but as you are only taking up nursing for a pastime, I sent for my niece and put her there, for she will take it up as a profession. You can do anything you like, but my niece stays there."

The girl was vexed at such treatment, so she walked away. She had only got to the foot of the stairs when she thought of the motive which led her into the hospital at first, and saying to herself, "My love for my country is a very poor thing if I cannot stand a little snub," she returned, and worked all night under the direction of this ignorant peasant woman, who had usurped her place.

When the doctors found it out, they placed the society girl in another and superior place, where she acquitted herself with honour.

It was very sad to me to witness the wrathful vindictive spirit that the war raised in my little charges. One of the illustrated papers had a picture of the baby children of the Crown Prince of Japan. Marie and Anastasie came running across to see the picture, and wanted to know who those queer little children were. I told them, and with a look of hatred coming into her sweet little face Marie slapped the picture with her open hand. "Horrid little people," said she; "they came and destroyed our poor ships and drowned our sailors." I explained to her that it was not these little children, who were only babies younger than Anastasie. So she said, "Yes; those little babies did it. Mama told me the Japs were all only little people."

Olga was working very diligently one day and said to me, "I hope the Russian soldiers will kill all the Japanese; not leave even one alive."

I told her there were many little children and women in Japan, people who could not fight, and asked her if she really thought it would be good of the Russian soldiers to kill them. She reflected for a moment, and then asked, "Have they an Emperor in Japan?" I answered, "Certainly." She asked various other questions which I answered; then she said slowly, "I did not know that the Japs were people like ourselves. I thought they were only like monkeys." She never said again anything about being pleased to hear of the deaths of the Japanese.

Someone in speaking to me of the four little girls lately said to me, "Olga has grace, wit, and good looks; Tatiana is a regular beauty; Marie is so sweet-natured, good and obliging, no one could help loving her; but little Anastasie has personal charm beyond any child I ever saw."

It was a good, and so far as it went, a true summary of the children as they would appear to a stranger, but there is a great deal more depth and strength of character in all the children than appears at first sight. I often wonder what use they will make of all the talents God has entrusted them with, and feel assured that as the apple never falls very far from the tree, so with such good parents my dear little charges will never go astray.

Chapter XXIII: The Russian Soldiers

THE Russian soldier looms at present very large on every horizon. Many a time have I seen Russian soldiers marching along to the regimental band, and when it stopped playing, singing choruses as they marched with vigour.

The Cossack regiments are most picturesque; they are magnificent horsemen and can stoop from the saddle and pick up any small article from the ground. Personally, I have always thought them slightly theatrical in costume, though their faces look martial enough for anything.

On holidays they wear long scarlet coats reaching nearly to the ankles, and top boots wrinkled at the legs. Their everyday uniform is a dark blue coat lined with scarlet. They are armed with silver-mounted swords, often heirlooms in their family, and wear a silver-mounted dagger in their belts, and they carry a rifle, the cartridges being slung across the breast of the coat. When the men are on horseback the rifle is carried across the saddle. The Cossacks are expert marksmen and can hit a target while going at full gallop. They are devoted to the Imperial family.

The Russian soldier receives board, lodgings, uniform and washing, and pocket-money at the rate of about one shilling per month. Out of this he has to provide himself with threads. He can, of course, earn a little more by doing odd jobs for his superiors, or acting as servant in an officer's family. I have frequently seen a private taking the children of an officer out for a walk. They are kindly handy creatures, and always seemed devoted to the little ones in their charge. The soldier receives his pocket-money every week, and generally puts by a little of it till he has saved about sixpence or eightpence. When he has this magnificent sum in his possession he indulges in his favourite amusement - i.e., he takes a street carriage and goes for a drive. Very funny and solemn he looks driving up and down the Nevsky.

No officer can live on his pay in Russia. A captain receives about twenty pounds per annum, which is not enough to dress him even. I myself know a general on half-pay; his income was just thirty pounds per annum and he had a wife and daughter to keep. In his youth he had painted pictures in watercolours. These he sold either in shops or to his friends, but his pictures had little or no merit, and became increasingly difficult to dispose of. When he rose to be a colonel his rank forbade him to try to sell his paintings, and so he bought a camera and eked out a miserable livelihood by photographing all sorts of scenes and selling the pictures. Amateur photographers were rare then, and for a while he did well. He used to be allowed to travel with the Imperial family and sent his photographs for reproduction in the newspapers; but he was old, unable for the fatigue of such a life, and was obliged to give it up. The Emperor gave him a flat with wood and light, and there this brave old soldier lives, with his wife and one daughter, on his thirty pounds per annum - a miserable life, indeed! He chose the wrong profession, one would say, but he still assures me that there is no life like the soldier's one, even without private means.

I once came into conflict with the military in Tsarskoe Selo. A room had been fitted up in the palace as a church, and the Empress and children attended Mass there on Sunday mornings. The Empress told me to get into the church by a little side-door, which would bring me just behind her chair, as all her three children were in church, and Marie Nicolaivna was so tiny a child that she might get restless. I went and found a soldier mounting guard outside the door; he refused to let me pass. I speak Russian very badly, and I tried to explain, but all to no purpose. So I waited and he stood and looked at me. Presently one of the Grand Dukes came along, and I explained the situation to him. He turned to the soldier, and he told him to let me pass. The soldier again refused, and the Grand Duke told him who he was. Of course, the man did not know him, and replied, "I don't care if you are the Emperor himself." The Grand Duke then asked him who had stationed him there, and the soldier replied, "My corporal, and without his permission I shall not allow anyone to pass through this door."

The Grand Duke then told me to wait for a few minutes, and he went off and found the corporal. The latter, when he came, was in a terrible rage. He seized the unfortunate soldier by the shoulders and began to shake him, but the Grand Duke interposed, told the corporal that the man was only doing his duty in obeying orders, and turning to the other complimented him highly, and said he was pleased to find that the soldiers were so obedient and so faithful to their orders. The poor soldier had tears in his eyes when the Grand Duke had finished speaking. Orders were given that in future I should be allowed to pass on giving my name.

On one occasion the Grand Duke Paul's children came to their own house at Tsarskoe Selo. A sentry was placed in the garden, but he did not know the children at all, and probably mistook the hour at which they were expected. He was dumbfounded when the children came running up and began to play in the sacred gymnasium and swing in the holy swings. He approached and said in his sternest tones, "What are you doing there? Don't you know that these gardens and all in them belong to Demitri and Marie Paulovitch?" Demitri mildly announced his identity, and the soldier said with great scorn, "Oh yes; it is very easy to say, 'I am the Grand Duke Demitri, but thou art a liar," using the familiar form of address. His distress was very great when he found that the children really belonged to the Imperial family.

When the war in the East broke out, it was very sad to see the soldiers marching off. I had never seen such a sight before, and to my eyes they looked so badly provided for such a long journey, but the trains provided for their use were exceedingly comfortable. The crossing of Lake Baikal seems to have been the worst part of the journey. The train moving across it broke down, as the ice was not strong enough for the traffic, so they went in sledges. Every few miles shelters were erected. The soldiers got hot coffee or soup and could thaw themselves at the fire before proceeding another stage. But even with these precautions some were frozen to death.

The Emperor got many thousands of letter-forms printed, and the children and I folded them, put them in envelopes, and stamped them - or many of them. The form of letter was something as follows: "My dear parents,- I am at___ In the battle of___; I was wounded in___ (or) I am ill in hospital; (or) I am in good health. How are___? Give my love to___." The blanks were to be filled in by a comrade who could write, or by a nurse. Many thousands of these letters were returned to cheer the hearts of the anxious relatives.

I was given a good many presents for the Empress's working party. A gentleman gave me five thousand roubles for the Empress; a lady gave me five hundred pounds of soap, and quantities of tow for the soldiers. There was a corridor at the Winter Palace packed with cases full of comforts for the soldiers. These were sent off every week, and we had the satisfaction of knowing that all we sent out arrived safely. But many strange stories were current as to the fate of the parcels sent from other working parties. One of the Grand Duchesses was head of the Red Cross Society, and had an enormous working party. She heard that when the boxes reached their destination they were half filled with rubbish. So the story goes that one evening, just before the train started for the East, she and one of her ladies went up to the station and insisted on examining the boxes. She found that the cases were half filled with stones and rubbish, with a layer of goods laid over them. I do not pretend to vouch for the truth of this story, but it was common talk in St. Petersburg and was never contradicted.

The Empress wished each soldier to receive a separate bundle for Easter, each containing one shirt, one handkerchief, one pair of socks, a set of bandages for the legs, one woollen cap, one parcel of tobacco with cigarette papers, one piece of soap and tow for washing, tea, coffee, sugar, notepaper and stamped envelopes, and a printed letterform.

Nearly everyone in the palace sent at least one such parcel, with the name and address of the donor inside, and many grateful letters were received from the recipients.

At the beginning of the war all nurses sent to the front were thoroughly trained, but later, when it became necessary to send more nurses, the authorities took almost all who volunteered, provided their health was good, gave them a short training-just six weeks in a military hospital - and sent them out. I saw one of these girls when she was ready to go out. She informed me that she had learned to read Latin, and could prescribe for patients as well as nurse them! All this in six weeks, and she had been a servant girl. Well, a few days in the hospital at the front would soon take that idea out of her.

Chapter XIV: Attacks on the Czar's Life

MANY false reports have been spread about attempts on the Emperor's life, but, nevertheless, a number of such attempts have been made. I have already spoken of one of them - the attempt to wreck the Imperial train when he was Czarovitch. Then he was travelling in Japan and a fanatic attacked him with a bludgeon. Prince George of Greece, his cousin, who was travelling with him, arrested the blow, but the Emperor got a nasty cut notwithstanding, and was laid up for a few days afterwards. He bears the mark on his forehead to this day. On the anniversary of that day there are thanksgiving services all through Russia, and the day is kept as a holiday throughout Russia.

The first year we were in the Crimea a diabolical plot against the Imperial family was formed, which was happily frustrated by the police. Had it been carried out the whole Court would have been dead and buried.

The grounds of Livadia are open to the public while the Imperial family are away. There was a priest in Yalta who used to like to stroll about among the vineyards and gardens, was exceedingly affable and kind, and showed a great curiosity regarding the daily life of the Emperor and family. He asked about the water supply, and even penetrated into the wood cellar. Before the Imperial family go into any town a police officer is sent to make enquiries regarding all in the place. On this occasion all were easily identified, with the exception of this priest. The police officer telegraphed to the town from which he said he came, and received an answer saying that all the priests belonging to the town were in charge of their churches. No one was absent, nor was anything known of him. One day when he was walking about Livadia the police entered his rooms. They found many in criminating papers, explosives, and even poisons. The explosives were destined for the wood cellar, and the poison for the water supply! It was fortunate for us that the springs in Livadia itself were dry that year, and the water was brought from a distance. The pseudo-priest was arrested and severely punished.

Another attempt was made some time before I went to Russia. The little church in Tsarskoe Selo had been altered, and was to be opened formally by Mass and a Te Deum. Just before divine service began a soldier discovered a bomb under a curtain just behind the Emperor and Empress's places in church. Had it exploded hundreds of persons would have perished.

The author of this horrible crime was a young man of university education. His mother had been early left a widow with this one child, a baby in arms. She was almost penniless when a housemaid in the palace heard of her, was moved with compassion towards her and her baby and gave her some white sewing to do. She interested others in the household in her sad case, and she was generously paid and helped.

She was shortly enabled to start a workroom with apprentices and got on well. When first she began, she used to carry her baby in her arms in and out of the palaces, and afterwards as he got bigger he used to fetch and carry work for her. He thus got to know all the palaces and the guards let him pass without trouble. He was well educated and entered the university. Here he became entangled in a secret society, and, owing to his intimate knowledge of the palaces, was chosen for the dreadful deed. He was arrested and confessed, but would not give the names of his accomplices. He was sent to Siberia for life. The shock of the affair killed his poor mother. The day he was arrested she died, as she said herself, of a broken heart at her son's baseness and ingratitude.

The last attempt on the Emperor was most subtle. A parcel posted at Suez was sent, marked "

Private." He received it while seated at tea with the Empress. On being opened it was found to contain a piece of dirty cloth, apparently cut from an old pair of trousers. He exclaimed in wonder at receiving such a curious thing. The Empress seized the tongs, and, taking the dirty cloth in them, sent it from the room. It was examined and found to be full of plague germs!

Much has lately been written regarding a constitution for Russia. It has come, but so far as I can judge, the people are not yet ready for it; not one in ten thousand understands the meaning of the word. A person fairly well educated was talking to me one time about the want of liberty in Russia. I told her that she could have very little more liberty in England than she had in Russia, being a woman and obliged to work for her living. I told her that the only liberty one could have was in keeping the laws and following them. She was greatly amazed, and asked me if we had laws in England; I replied, "Certainly; and those who break them speedily find themselves in prison." "What," she exclaimed, "prisons in free England!" She went on to ask what was forbidden to people in England, and was greatly amazed when I gave her a list. She told me she would not go any more to see those people who had been telling her she was only a slave.

Employers of labour in Russia are in many instances obliged to hire workers from day to day. The Russian workmen do not like to continue to work for a whole week right off; no matter what the press of business may be, they will suddenly announce that they are tired and want a holiday, and go off for two or three days without even finishing the job in hand.

The proprietor of some petroleum wells in the Caucasus told me this story. He had been called upon to settle a strike, and came over from London for the purpose. He saw the men, who submitted a list of claims. Shorter hours, more pay, and a supply of water for drinking purposes, being the chief things. The last item in their list of grievances was, "We do not like an autocratic sovereign." He told them that the water supply was being brought as quickly as possible. He added five kopecks (about one penny-farthing per day) to their wages, and took an hour off the day's work. "And as for the last thing", he said, "'It shall have my most earnest consideration.'" It was rather puzzling to know what these poor workers expected of their employer, or how they looked to be benefited by a constitution.

It is only a little more than forty years since Alexander II freed the slaves. It was a noble action, but it might have been more beneficial had it been done in a different manner. It is, of course, very easy to be wise after the event, and in this case no one could foresee the event.

The poor peasants were slaves in the morning and freed men in the evening. All house servants were turned out, field labourers and working men were let loose, and committed the most awful excesses. Many of the house servants returned to their masters and begged to be taken back in their homes. To this day in some households there are old men and women slaves, not receiving any wages, but working for their keep, and receiving clothing from the hands of their masters and mistresses.

In consequence of the extreme misery and famine which fell on the country through the madness of these poor freed slaves, laws were passed, binding the peasant to the land ill which he was born. A peasant could leave his district only after complying with very stringent regulations, and paying a sum of money to the Starosta, or Elder. Two years ago the Emperor proclaimed that these peasants were henceforth free to leave their villages and go where they liked. I do not know that many availed themselves of this permission, however.

Russia has a kind of local government, but until the people are better educated it seems to me that a constitution cannot benefit them much. They are not capable of guiding themselves. The little nursery party in Tsarskoe Selo would be just as well able to arrange their daily life without the aid of "grown-ups" as are the Russians in general.

What they do want, and want badly, is clean hands in the executive.

During the past forty years Russia has made gigantic strides towards civilisation. In the matter of higher education for women she is well abreast of the times. In St. Petersburg and Moscow, and, in fact, all the great centres, there are hundreds of women working as doctors, chemists, dentists, and even finding employment in banks. Russian industries are protected by a high tariff. Buy an article in England and have it sent to you, and you will find that you pay about as much again in Custom House duties as the thing cost in England.

Under this system Russian industries are advancing. Linen is almost as good as that produced in Ireland, but cottons and woollen materials fall very far behind our own productions, which are, however, prohibitory in prices to all with limited means. I have myself seen ordinary English pique sold in Russia for four and sixpence the archine (about three-quarters of a yard), while Russian pique can be had for about ten pence.

Chapter XV: Social Life in Russia

SOCIAL life is much simpler than in England. At theatres and dinners in public places, hotels, restaurants, and so forth, afternoon dress is considered de rigueur. No one would think of putting on a décolleté gown. It would be considered very bad form. At theatres, however, both in the morning and evening, hats are removed as an act of courtesy to those seated behind. At all small parties, whether dinner, dancing, or music, or small games, a light silk, muslin or canvas dress, made high, is worn.

But at all big functions full dress is worn. At a Court luncheon a low-necked dress and a large picture hat is the costume. Men, however, unless in uniform, wear evening dress oftener than with us. A music master will give his lessons in the regulation evening suit. It looks very funny.

On the first of January all men drive round to their acquaintances in full evening dress, congratulate the ladies, and are supposed to drink to their health. For this they put on evening dress. They start about nine o'clock in the morning, so it looks rather peculiar. Poor fellows! They come home in the evening generally worn out, very hungry, and with a raging headache, born of all the sips of vodki taken during the day.

Nine o'clock in the evening is a favourite time for paying visits. At this hour the Russians drink tea; the tray is brought in and glasses of tea are dispensed without cream or milk, but very sweet, and with slices of lemon floating in each glass, or, if preferred, a spoonful of jam is stirred into the glass. They looked upon me as a heathen, because I don't take sugar in tea.

A sister of mine was visiting on a farmhouse in the north of Ireland once, and said to the hostess, "Please, no sugar for me." She looked surprised, but answered encouragingly, "Oh, Mrs. H., we have plenty of sugar in the house." Well, that did not happen to me in Russia, but much surprise was expressed at my want of taste. Russians will sometimes hold a lump of sugar in their fingers and nibble a bit of it before taking a mouthful of tea. They say it tastes better so.

The tea-table is always well furnished with cakes of various kinds, some of them particularly nasty. I used to think they were flavoured with hair-oil. Caraway and poppy seeds are all largely used in confectionery; fruit and bonbons are also served with tea.

The tea equipage is generally very dainty; the glasses are put into silver stands with handles to enable them to be lifted with ease; pretty gilt or enamelled silver is used, and the napery is of the finest, most dainty description, for Russians love fine linen. Every Russian has his or her own store of linen, just as he has his own underclothing, and I have heard much wonder expressed at the bare idea of sleeping on the sheets and pillow covers of other people. Even a servant brings her own house-linen with her.

When a layette is prepared sheets and towels, etc., are always included, and kept separate for each child's use, and it is counted very careless to put the sheets of one child in the bed of another. In going on a visit anywhere, you take your own sheets, etc., with you, and send them to the wash with your own linen. English people, however, are excused from this, on account of their incomprehensible habit of using family linen. But if a Russian governess or visitor's linen is not up to the mark, she receives very scornful looks from the servants.

In the trains, for a night journey one can either bring sheets, blankets and a pillow, or hire from the conductor for one rouble - about two shillings. But soap or towels are never provided.

The following story is told of an Englishman travelling for the first time in Russia. He met a Russian who spoke all languages, and confided to him that he had brought no towel, and was tired of wiping his face on his sheet or pocket-handkerchief, and he could not succeed in making the conductor understand what he wanted. The Russian told him he had only to say "Politiensa," and his wants would be supplied. The Englishman learned the word, and presently called for the conductor, and, as he thought, asked for a towel.

The conductor gesticulated and bowed, but brought no towel, so the Englishman gave it up. Later on he met his Russian friend, and told him that though he had said what he had been told he had got no towel. "Stupid man!" said he; "can't even understand his own language." The Russian caned the conductor and spoke to him. He turned to the Englishman and asked him what he had said. The latter replied,

112

"Palatinski, of course." Judge of his surprise when he heard that he had actually asked the poor conductor if he spoke Latin. The latter had replied that he only spoke Russian and German, and excused himself for not knowing Latin by saying it was so seldom called for.

Duelling is still a recognised institution in the land of the Tsar. One of the officers about the Court is said to have fought three, and killed his man each time. I always felt a horror of the man, but I believe, notwithstanding his bloody record, he was quite harmless and even good-natured.

On one occasion a young officer of a Cossack regiment took two girls from a cafe chantant to spend a day in the country. In the evening all three, being heated with wine, made their way to the station; the women entered the train and the prince stood on the platform talking to a friend. The women had seated themselves opposite a gentleman who had a terrible scar on his face, the result of a sword-cut which had laid open his visage from temple to chin.

The two women began to make impertinent and offensive remarks about the man and his appearance. They were French and spoke in their own language. He at last replied to them in French: "Ladies, when first you got into the train I thought you were French ladies; I now see I was mistaken. French ladies are too delicate in sentiment, and too polite to mock at a scar won in honourable warfare. I now perceive that you are nothing but a pair of peasants." He got up and went to another part of the train, leaving the women speechless under his well-merited rebuke.

When the prince got into the train the women told him that they had been insulted, described the appearance of the gentleman, and urged him to challenge him for a duel. The prince accordingly sought him out and gave him his card, saying, "You have insulted mes dames and must fight a duel."

Now the other was a retired military man, who had fought for the Boers against England. He had also been through the Turkish war, and had seventeen wounds on his body. After the war in South Africa was over he had returned to Russia and taken up journalism as a profession. He had no wish to fight a duel, and replied to the effect that he had seen rivers of blood flow, had the scars of seventeen wounds on his body, and no one, therefore, could call his courage into question. He would not fight, specially for two such women as those. He was a journalist, and only desired peace.

The prince returned to his companions. When the train arrived in St. Petersburg the journalist was the last person to alight, but his enemies were waiting outside the station for him. As he approached, one woman pushed her companion against him violently. He caught her by the arms and steadied her or she would have fallen, and he then tried to pass on. But the prince blocked his way. Forcing his card on him he demanded his address and satisfaction. In the course of the evening two friends of the prince called upon the journalist. The latter again refused to fight, but said that the officer owed him an apology. This, of course, was refused. Now an officer cannot fight a duel without permission from his general, and at the moment the latter was in Krasnoe Selo in attendance on the Emperor, who was there for manoeuvres.

When he returned he found himself unable to come to any decision, and the matter was referred to the Emperor, who gave permission for the duel to take place. The place of meeting was just outside Peterhoff, where we were residing at the moment. Lots were drawn, and the prince had the first shot. He aimed for the scar in the journalist's face but missed him by a hair's breadth. The journalist, wishing to wound his antagonist slightly, aimed low, intending to inflict a flesh wound in the thigh; but the pistol carried too high, and the bullet entered the abdomen, inflicting a mortal wound. The journalist, full of horror, threw down his pistol, and going up to his foe asked his forgiveness, saying, he had no intention of inflicting so severe a punishment. The dying man refused to shake hands, and cursed him bitterly. Shortly afterwards he expired.

His younger brother took up the quarrel, and sent a challenge to the journalist; but there was absolutely no ground for a second duel, and permission was refused.

During the winter the journalist was picked up in an unconscious state in the streets of St. Petersburg, and was carried to the hospital. He was terribly injured. He rallied a little, and declared that the younger brother of the man he had shot had entered his flat after midnight, accompanied by three friends, and had thrown him from the window in revenge. He died a couple of days after. The prince and his friends on their part denied the truth of the whole story, and said that the journalist had had a card-party in his rooms on the evening in question; a dispute had arisen, and he was thrown from the window by his own friends. But no evidence on the point was forthcoming, and the journalist's own servant knew nothing about the card-party. The unfortunate man's rooms showed signs of a terrible struggle. No inquiry into the truth of either story was made; the authorities accepted the living man's story, and the matter ended.

Another very terrible thing happened while I was in Russia. A German oculist settled in St. Petersburg. He was clever and skilful, and speedily got a great practice. He was a bachelor, and his sister kept house for him. At the time of my story both were middle-aged, and enjoyed a very good reputation.

He made the acquaintance of a rather fast officer, who had a pretty wife. This acquaintance soon ripened into a close intimacy, and visits were frequently exchanged between the two families. One morning during the doctor's reception hours the officer came to his house and asked to see him for a moment. The servant, knowing him to be an intimate friend of his master, arranged for him to slip in as soon as the patient with whom the oculist was at that moment engaged should be free. At the moment the waiting-room was full of patients who were speedily startled by the report of a revolver, quickly followed by another. The servant rushed into the room and found his master lying wounded on the floor.

The officer, saying calmly, "I have shot your master, you will find me in my own house should you want me," went out. The police were speedily on the spot. Inquiries were set on foot and the officer was placed under arrest in his own house.

Though dying, the oculist was quite conscious, and told the following story: When the officer came into the room he at once accused his friend of being on too intimate terms with his wife; but, he added that if the oculist would promise to marry her, and give him, the aggrieved husband, a considerable sum of money, he would allow his wife to divorce him, and offer no obstacle, in order that she might be free to marry the man of her choice. His wife's good name and happiness were the most cherished objects of his life. The oculist refused to accept these terms. The officer then suggested the money without the wife, who was, he said, so dear to him that he would forgive her anything.

The oculist declared that he was absolutely innocent of the offence, and proposed an enquiry.

On this, without a word of warning, the officer drew a revolver from his pocket and shot the other across the table. He was wounded in the thigh and fell to the ground; the officer just fired a second shot into the prostrate body when the servant came into the room.

The officer's story was that he challenged the oculist to a duel which was refused, and he then fired at him, that being duelling etiquette in Russia. The oculist lingered for two or three days, but maintained to the last hour that he was innocent of this charge. The St. Petersburg priests took up the matter warmly, and said that the officer was justified in shooting down the man who had desecrated his home, so there was no enquiry into the matter and the officer was set at liberty.

But the authorities thought the air of St. Petersburg not good for the pretty wife, and she went down to a country town, a good long way from St. Petersburg. Here the couple speedily made acquaintance with a very wealthy young man, on whom they showered invitations, and who was soon established as "l'ami de la maison." In fact, so confiding was the officer that he would invite him to the house to amuse his wife while he was on duty, or at his club. Madame was very fascinating. She liked the things on sale in the local shops so much; their young friend knew the town so well, could he not escort her and show her shops? Of course, he did so. Madame was unlucky about her purses; she lost quite a number, and the young man generally settled up with a cheque.

One evening when the officer and his wife were both at home and alone the police paid them a visit and requested them to move on, which they accordingly did, to the great joy of all the decent inhabitants of that town. They tried the same game in another town to which they went, but were pulled up in time by the police.

Throughout Russia the flat system prevails. Some houses contain forty or fifty sets of apartments, and you can get a flat of any size you want, from two rooms to fifteen or sixteen. The authorities put a man called a "dvornik" into each house; he is a sort of inferior policeman. He keeps the road and footpath in front of the house swept and clean - the streets of St. Petersburg are beautifully kept – and knows all who pass in and out of the house, tells the police should anyone come into the house on a visit, and is responsible for the safety of all in the house.

Should a burglary or a murder be committed, he is punished, generally by being sent to the country in disgrace. I must say they do their duty very well, and one seldom hears of burglaries or murders being committed in St. Petersburg, and such crimes as one hears of in London, such as mysterious disappearances, murders in common lodging houses, girls decoyed into low houses, etc., are never heard of in Russia.

During the six years I lived in the Russian capital there was one double murder committed. In broad daylight, in one of the very best parts of the town quite close to the Winter Palace, an old lady and her servant were murdered and the flat was rifled. The authors of the terrible crime were never discovered.

Chapter XVI: Post Office Vagaries in Russia

PUBLIC offices in Russia seem to me to be in sore need of reform. In a little country post office which in this country would be managed and well looked after by a postmistress, one finds three great men in charge. Of course they have a great deal more to do there than here and give themselves a lot of perfectly unnecessary trouble in reading the letters entrusted to the care of the government.

I write a very illegible hand and used to pity them trying to decipher my writing, hampered in addition with a foreign language. Last autumn a lady belonging to the Court wrote a letter to the Empress while she was in Poland. She sealed it and even wrote her name outside the envelope, which is supposed to ensure the letter going through without examination.

A couple of days afterwards the letter was returned to her from the post office with an intimation that it had opened of itself in the post office. The seal was intact but had been detached probably by means of a knife. It was, of course, the merest curiosity which led them to open this letter. As a general rule the police open one letter in every fifteen passing through the post office. Should they injure the envelope they at once put the letter into the fire and it is done with. In times of national danger a much larger proportion of letters are opened and read. Again, judging by stories one hears, the postmen themselves cannot be depended upon. A friend of mine told me that on one occasion she saw a postman open the stove in an entrance hall and calmly burn a number of letters. I wanted to know why she did not report him and she said it could not have done any good. Till the people have a keener sense of right and wrong she seemed to think a mere report would do no good, but I think I should have tried it all the same.

This year an old friend of mine sent me through the post some Irish crotchet; she enclosed a note in her parcel. This note was delivered to me minus stamp or postmark. I sent down at once to enquire about the lace but was told that the letter had come as I received it, straight from County Cork without post-mark or stamp; but as I did not seem to be satisfied they would not make any charge for it! The envelope was not marked in any way. Somebody in the post office evidently admired the lace and kept it. Gloves or any small thing sent through post were never delivered to me unless the sender took the precaution of registering the letter.

On an average I lost about twenty letters in the year. I was told that all letters coming from the palace were opened, so I found it better if possible to get mine posted in a pillar box in the street. In the country, of course, I could not do this, but used sometimes to send my letters to St. Petersburg to be posted. On one occasion I registered a letter to an address in Cornwall; it took me at least a week to get that letter posted, as the officials in the country post office were absolutely certain that Cornwall was in America and would not take the letter because I had written England on it. At last I sent the letter to St. Petersburg and told the messenger simply to hand it in and say nothing about its destination unless asked, when he could ask the official to write London across it and register it as far as London and then let it take its chance.

The letter was refused; so then my messenger made my proposal to have it registered to London and said I was certain that Cornwall was in England; the official thereupon took the letter and registered it but he said if it went astray he would not be accountable for it. They had protested against it but the sender would not heed. Some ten or twelve days afterwards they sent me word that the letter had been received. The postal guide must have been wrong in locating Cornwall in America.

On one occasion a London firm sent a parcel by post to the Grand Duchesses; it was not received. I had all enquiries made but it was lost. I accordingly told the Empress and she made enquiries about it.

An official was sent up to the palace. He saw the Empress, who sent him to me. He began by assuring me that he was an Englishman and giving me his solemn word of honour which I might believe, as an Englishman never lies. He then proceeded to tell me that I had made an enemy in the Berlin post office and that this monster of iniquity stole my letters in Berlin. Now it so happens that I never stayed even a night in Berlin and have no acquaintance whatsoever with the town or people. I told him so, whereupon he offered to swear to me that the letters were not lost in Russia; as he was an Englishman I might believe him! I noticed that many English people used to bribe officials in the post office to deliver their letters without letting the police see them, or at least they said they did and would talk quite openly about its being impossible to get on in Russia without bribing. Somehow in Russia it is looked on in quite a different light from what it is in England, and I used to be laughed at because I always maintained that morality was the same for all countries, that if it was wrong to try to buy justice and right in one country it surely was equally wrong in another. But the fact of its being punishable in one country and not in another made no difference in such a matter as that.

I told this particular Englishman that he might read my letters, if he chose, so long as he gave them to me afterwards, there never was anything in them but family news of no interest to anyone but myself. He was horrified at this suggestion of mine and exclaimed, "God forbid and the Emperor has forbidden that we should touch your letters," so I said, "God may forbid and the Emperor has forbidden you to touch my letters, still they are lost all the same," and went on to play a game of bluff with him by telling him that most of my letters came from England and Ireland and were therefore under the International Postal Law, and that I very much doubted if he had any legal right to touch them at all. He told me I had opened a very interesting legal point which would have his consideration and took his leave; but the letters continued to be lost all the same. If I was really anxious about a letter I used to post it open or only just closed, which I found was a very good plan.

On one occasion I ordered a copy of Morfill's History of Russia, as I felt interested in it. Judge of my amazement at hearing that it was forbidden to circulate it in Russia. I however asked special permission for it and so got it after a little delay without further trouble. The censor's office keeps books sometimes for months. A friend of mine sent me a book he had written as a Christmas present; it was Easter before I got it and then it had evidently been given to a child to play with, for it was scribbled over in red and blue pencil.

State censorship of the press is a very good thing and in my opinion the English press would benefit greatly by it as would also the American, but one can have too much of a good thing. It is not the law to which one objects but the methods in which it is carried out. This is equally true of both the free press and the censored one.

Some time ago in St. Petersburg the censor discovered that postcards were sold openly in the capital with such wicked devices as pictures of St. Isaac's Cathedral, the Nevski Perspective, or the Winter Palace, but without the magic words "Censor's Permit" in the corner of each card; he immediately prohibited the sale of these awful cards and for about ten days none were permitted to be sold. Now it so happened that I wanted some of these cards and went into a shop to get them. The proprietor politely told me he could not sell them. Greatly amazed, I exclaimed, "But why! they are in your window." He was exceedingly angry and told me of the censor's prohibition. I thought, naturally enough, that there was some suspicion attaching to the man himself and left the shop. I went to another, only to meet with the same story, and to a third, where they offered to sell them to me sub rosa and begged me to send them under cover as the sale had been prohibited. I however refused to buy under these circumstances and never again entered the shop. The strange part of this censorship is that with it frightfully indecent pictures and cards are openly shown in the windows and shops, and one has to be careful as to what theatre one goes to, for some of the plays are absolutely repulsive, violating every canon of good taste, decency and modesty.

But with a little time these things will all right themselves; when education has spread more amongst the people and they are more elevated they will see for themselves that these things do not become a great Christian people, and they will be relegated to oblivion with many other things which all lovers of the country must deplore.

Chapter XXVII: The True Story of Kishineff

MUCH has been written concerning the outrages at Kishineff which is absolutely untrue. It is far from my intention to deny the facts of the matter.

Atrocities which could not have been surpassed by the Spanish Inquisition were committed on a defenceless and unarmed population, but neither the Emperor nor the Russian government was to blame in the matter.

The first intimation I had of it was from the London Times. I read the accounts with deep horror and asked some Russian friends of mine if it could possibly be true, but no one seemed to know anything about it, though one of them searched the Russian papers. She could find no mention of it in them. A few days later accounts of the horrible outrage were published in the Russian papers; an inquiry was made and those upon whom guilt rested were severely punished.

Two Russians in the town of Kishineff were guardians to their orphan nephew, a lad of about fourteen years of age. He was rich, his father having made a fortune; his uncles, who were his heirs at law, having got into financial difficulties, hit upon the abominable project of murdering the poor boy and annexing his wealth. The lad returned from school one day and was never seen alive again. It was just at the time of the Jewish Passover and the uncles informed the police of the disappearance of the nephew, adding their belief that the Jews had taken his blood for ritual purposes, for that old myth is largely believed in Russia.

The police instituted a search in the Jewish quarters for the unfortunate lad and with the assistance of the uncles soon found the body, which had been quite drained of blood, in the garden of a Jew.

The Christian population was much inflamed against the unhappy Jews, who were, of course, unable to give proofs of their absolute innocency in the matter.

Jew baiting is a form of sport only too common in Russia; so a terrible vengeance was planned; word was sent to all the Jews in the neighbourhood that as they had for their Passover Feast taken the blood of a Christian so would the Christians pour out to their God on Easter the blood of the Jews. The rich Jews in the town went to the governor and besought his protection. They paid for it too with all their possessions.

On Easter Sunday morning a guard was placed outside their houses and they were warned not to stir out, but no help or protection was given to the poor Jews whose houses were entered; their children were thrown from the windows and dashed to pieces against the walls and pavements. One young man was nailed to a rude cross in the streets and had all his limbs sawn off; the horrors of hell were let loose upon the most unhappy people. The very worst barbarities committed in the Middle Ages were exceeded.

It was, of course, the duty of the governor to call out the military and protect the helpless, but he had been paid in advance, and wished to earn his money; therefore he deliberately cut off all telephone communication, shut himself up in his study, and would give no answer to anyone.

The military authorities went several times to his house for permission to suppress the rioting, but could not get any answer. Like the deaf adder he would not hear, neither did he send any report of the matter to St. Petersburg and the Russians absolutely believed that they were fulfilling the Emperor's desires. In the evening the Russians returned to their houses satisfied with themselves and their work; their horror may be imagined when they found they were to be brought to justice for their terrible doings, for they imagined they had been doing the will of God and the Emperor's orders.

The enquiry into the outrages lasted a long time; the police searched the house of the uncles and found in a cellar plenty of evidence to prove that the poor boy had met his death in his own home; the very clothes which he had worn at school on the last day of his life, the weapon with which the murder had been committed, and many more mute witnesses being found. The wretched uncles were justly punished by being sent to Siberia for life. The ringleaders in the attack on the Jews were sentenced to varying terms of imprisonment, from two years to a few months, according to their degree of guilt, but a terrible punishment was reserved for the most guilty of all, the governor. All his property was confiscated and he was deprived of his passport and sent to live in a village; in other words, he was outlawed and he is, in the eyes of the law, dead. He can neither write nor receive letters and to support his miserable life he was obliged to take service in a peasant's family and be the general drudge. If they wish, they may beat, kick, starve him and he has no redress.

This man has no land and no rights from anyone. His master will give him food, a sheep-skin coat for winter and a corner of the floor to sleep on at night; he may not go beyond about a mile from the village in any direction. Yet he was a gentleman used to a soft, luxurious life. Russia can inflict no worse punishment than this, but it is very seldom given; I have heard of men condemned to this sentence of outlawry running away and hiding in the woods and becoming "wild men" who stick at no crime; of course, wanting a passport they cannot enter any other village or town and so they will sometimes murder a whole family in order to steal this precious document which must often be utterly useless to them, as a description of the personal appearance of the owner is written in each Russian passport.

Chapter XXVIII: The Russian Clergy

THE RUSSIAN CLERGY. THE Greek Church, which is established in Russia, is supposed to hold a place between the Protestant and Roman Catholic churches; it is, however, in ritual and doctrine, more like the latter than the former, though orthodox Russians as a rule prefer Protestants to Roman Catholics. The Greek Church denies the supremacy of the Pope, its clergy are married, Mass is sung in the vulgar tongue, and it does not hold the doctrine of the Immaculate conception.

Many of the priests are excellent men, working hard for the good of their people and leading self-sacrificing lives, true ornaments to the Christian profession; on the other hand, many of them seem to be devoid of any sense of morality. In many respects their lives are very sad, they are so cut off from all others. They are simply peasants and to the level of peasants their younger sons often sink, consequently they are not received into any society. Their education, training and priestly office lift them above the level of the mere tiller of the fields who looks upon the priests with a sort of superstitious awe on Sundays, but on whose life they exercise no influence whatever. The eldest son, or priest, is set apart for the priesthood and no military service is required of him, but the younger sons frequently serve as common soldiers. The groom who led little Anastasie Nicolaivna's donkey was the son of a priest and no one considered it at all an extraordinary thing that he should serve in the stables; in fact, he was considered as being very lucky to have got such a good position and so pleasant a life. He had served as a private in the army and could read and write.

A priest is obliged to marry before he receives orders; his wife is in many cases chosen for him by the bishop; should she die he has to give up his charge, take leave of his children, and go into a monastery, a second marriage being absolutely forbidden to him and a priest without a wife is not allowed to live in a parish. From the monasteries promotion comes. What the life is there I cannot tell but it must be frightfully monotonous. The brothers do a great deal of wood-carving, some of which is very beautiful. In all the monasteries one can buy for a few pence little wooden spoons carved by the brothers; these have all got "A sign of the blessing" on the top. The right hand is extended, the first and second fingers joined to the thumb and the other two fingers turned in. I have several of these spoons in my possession; I always thought it such a pity to shut up men of education, who might labour for the welfare of their fellow creatures in a monastery, to eat out their lives carving wooden spoons, but the Russian Church moves very slowly. While I was in Russia a conference was held to discuss the desirability of altering the calendar, which is thirteen days behind the rest of the world, but the Church would not hear of it, alleging that a Christian feast, such as Easter, should not be kept on the same day as the Jewish Passover!

Priests' daughters are educated at excellent institutes set aside for themselves.

On the completion of the education of a priest's daughter, should she not be already engaged, her photograph is taken and sent to all the theological schools to be inserted in the public album. On the back are written full particulars as to her height, age, parentage, fortune, number of brothers and sisters, etc. Should a man not have formed any previous engagement, on the passing of his final examination he goes to the album and looks up two or three suitable candidates for matrimonial bliss, writes to the fathers of the chosen few and an interview is arranged for. When suited, he writes to the fathers of the others, and tells them on whom his choice has fallen and no one is any the worse. Should his wife's father die, he takes his mother-in-law to live with him.

While I was in St. Petersburg a priest died and left four unmarried daughters; in accordance with the usual custom the bishop appointed to the vacant charge a young man whose affections were free, and it was supposed that he would marry one of the daughters and provide for their mother. One after the other of these brave girls refused his offer, not that they had anything against the man, but they said they wished to have some choice in the matter and did not wish to marry where they did not love.

They left their father's house and taking their mother with them they started a school where they are doing well. I sympathised deeply with them and spoke to a Russian lady of their courage in thus defying convention and starting out in the world for themselves. She, however, took quite another view of the matter and said, "What do they suppose they have been brought up and educated for; it was their plain duty to marry priests and I have no patience with people who will not perform their duty. Where are priests to look for wives if priests' daughters refuse to marry them?"

If a priest has daughters and no son, he has to educate a young man for the sacred office in order to marry him to one of his daughters; should he have no children at all he is obliged to adopt a son.

The Empress is doing all in her power to raise the social standing of the priests and to provide them with a settled income.

When a Russian family visits Holy Moscow it is considered correct to hire a priest to say matins, and accordingly a servant-man is sent to the market-place to hire. The priests stand there, each one with a little roll of bread in his hand. The servant chooses his man, and then begins the horrible bartering without which it seems impossible to conclude any bargain. The priest will ask perhaps five or six roubles; the servant will endeavour to get him cheaper. Should the priest be getting the worst of the encounter he will sometimes say something like this: "If you won't give me my price I'll take a bite of this bread, and then it will all be done," for a priest cannot celebrate mass unless he is fasting. Should the servant be new to the business he will probably give in and conclude the bargain; but if he is wide awake he will answer something like this: "For that matter you may eat it all. There are plenty more priests in the market." But suppose the bargain concluded! On the conclusion of matins the priest holds up the cross and all the worshippers press forward to kiss it and the hand of the priest, who is then sent to the kitchen to breakfast with the servants.

It is related of the late Emperor that being in the country for military manoeuvres he attended divine service in the village church. On the conclusion of the Mass he advanced to kiss the cross and the priest's hand. The latter withdrew his hand, saying, "It is not meet that your Majesty should kiss the hand of his humble servant." The Emperor reproved him in these words: "Thou fool, it is not thy hand I kiss but the holy office thou holdest. I do it not for thee but for my people."

Holy pictures and relics hold a great place in the Russian Church. In the cathedral in the Winter Palace is a dried human hand. It is very old. Tradition says that it is the hand of John the Baptist!

Holy pictures may be either painted or carved, but are always hand-work, though they may only cost a few kopecks each. The Russian never speaks of buying or selling these pictures. They are always exchanged. Exchanging for money is not the same thing as buying, they say.

Some pictures are used something like charms. There is one of three saints, Iger, Saumon, and Ivava. With this image engaged couples are usually blessed by their parents before the marriage. If an unengaged person is given the image, he or she is certain, so the fable goes, of being married before the year is over. I gave a copy of it to a girl three years ago but it had no effect; she is still living in single blessedness. I told her she must have failed in faith. As a matter of fact, moved by some feeling of shyness, she shut up the picture in a box and never put it in her little shrine at all. She carried it about with her from place to place, but I really do not think she gave it very fair play. She was a little ashamed of having locked it up, and never could make out whether I had given it to her in jest or seriousness.

One of the Russian nurses got engaged while I was there. When we were last in Moscow she came to me and told me that she had dreamt that an angel came to her and said, "If you wish to be happy in your marriage you must get an icon of Iger, Saumon, and Ivava." She told the angel that she had numbers of holy pictures, would not one of the Madonna do instead?"

But the angel was of a different opinion and said nothing would do but what he had pointed out.

Of course, I told her that if her married happiness depended upon that, to go and get as many as ever she wished; so she dressed and went.

Shortly afterwards the Empress came into the nurseries and asked for her. I told her she had gone out to buy something she required. So the Empress asked me to send the girl to her as soon as she returned. She then showed me a copy of this picture, saying, "It is supposed to bring luck and happiness to brides, I saw it in a church I was visiting and brought it home for her." It was a curious coincidence.

In 1903 a new saint was added to the Russian calendar - St. Seraphim. He was a monk, and was remarkable for the great gentleness and piety of his character. He lived in a monastery situated in a forest. He is generally represented with a great bear which he had tamed, and which followed him about like a dog. He was deformed. Wandering in the forest one day he was attacked and beaten by a ruffian; his back was broken, but he recovered and lived for some years. Many extraordinary stories are related of him. He only died about seventy-five years ago, but owing to his extraordinary piety, he was canonized far sooner than is usual.

The Emperor and Empress went to the ceremony. They were lodged in the convent there, their suite being accommodated either in the stables, where beds were made up, or in tents. But for the most part the pilgrims, numbering about one and a half millions, slept in the forest or in the grounds of the monastery with the sky for a canopy. The monks were not at all prepared for such numbers, and there was not nearly sufficient bread, or food of any kind, to go round. Many apparently authentic cures are recorded; the blind received their sight, the lame walked, but I cannot say if the cures were permanent.

Talking of them with a Russian doctor, he said he had no doubt whatever of the truth of certain of these cures, but he believed they were all of the nervous system; but then nervous diseases are the most difficult of all to cure. One cure is reported of a young girl suffering from typhoid whose people had taken a cottage in the neighbourhood for the summer. One morning her mother was horrified to find her bed empty. Search was immediately made all over the house and the garden, but she could not be found. Suddenly she walked into the house, quite well, and asked for breakfast. She told the following story:

In the night a little old man appeared to her, and told her to get up and go and bathe in a spring of water, several miles distant from the house. She protested, saying she had been in bed for several weeks and had not strength enough to walk downstairs, but the apparition said, "Only obey, strength will be given to thee, only have faith." She got up, walked to the spring and bathed, and was quite restored, nor had she a relapse.

On these remarkable circumstances being made known, it was resolved to canonize St. Seraphim, and I am sure that he merited the distinction, owing to the beauty of his life and character.

The Bible tells us that if we have faith all things are possible to us, so I believe that these miracles were worked in answer to faith. Many people walked from Archangel on the White Sea down to the monastery, which is situated in the south of Russia, starting, like the apostles of old, without provision for the journey. Many people were walking for six months.

Two brothers set out carrying their paralysed sister in a stretcher between them and made their way on foot to the shrine. Their journey took them over five months. They begged their way; underwent in credible hardships. Starting on their long, toilsome journey in March, when every place was frozen hard, they travelled on through snow, under the burning sun, still carrying their helpless sister, sustained by the hope of a blessing for her. Their faith was rewarded. Their sister was restored. Charitable people helped them to return home by train. They had the three greatest things in the world, faith, hope and charity, and they were rewarded.

Chapter XXIX: More about the Children

THE Russian peasants live principally on rye. When this crop fails ruin and starvation stare them in the face.

The following story was told me of the effects of eating rye in a bad condition. The scenes described took place in a village not far from Moscow. The poorest people ground the unripe, rotten grain, and made it into a travesty of the black bread which they usually use. This bread was rankly intoxicating and the poor creatures who ate it were absolutely insane for a while. They danced naked through the villages, attacked each other with knives, screaming like savages the while. Even little children were made drunk. Many died, falling down suddenly in the midst of their frenzy. Generally speaking, after about two hours of this excitement the poor creatures dropped off into a sudden and profound sleep, from which they woke sober and in their right minds. Many, alas! Awoke no more.

The Russian peasants dislike loneliness very much, and always live in - villages; sometimes their cabins may be forty miles from their farms. During the summer they generally camp out, shutting up the cabin, the peasant, his wife and family travelling in a rough cart, traverse the distance between house and farm.

They generally plough with a woman or two and a cow, and the man drives this extraordinary team. I often said if I were those women I should strike. My nephew says it is unscriptural, for it is forbidden to yoke an ox and an ass! I told a peasant woman once that I considered it awful, and she laughed and said, "Eta nichivo" "It is no matter."

In harvest time they work far into the night, for in the north of Russia daylight lingers long. One can see to read up to about ten o'clock at night without artificial light, and they work even by moonlight cutting grass, binding sheaves, etc. The harvest is carried home and stored, the cattle are driven back to the village, and the long sad winter begins. The summer spent out of doors is certainly good for the children, who run about sturdy, brown, little, half-naked savages.

One of the under-nurses in the Imperial household had a friend who lived in a village with her mother; the friend did the Russian drawn thread work most beautifully. I saw some of it one day, and sent her an order. I showed it to several people and got her orders. I even sent a good deal of it to England and Ireland, and got her better prices than she had got from the shops for articles she had worked. She was soon enabled to take in a couple of girls as apprentices, and had a little establishment. Her cottage was comfortable, and she and her mother lived in a degree of comfort which they had not before known. One day the maid came to tell me that her friend was married and could do no work. I thought it rather a pity for her to give up her work, as the Russian winters are long, and I thought she would find time hang heavily on her hands and said so. The girl said she could not work at present, as she was too tired in the evening when she was finished ploughing. I was amused, and said I had never heard of a woman driving the plough, and she then told me she was not driving, but dragging it with a cow.

I said I supposed she must have been very fond of the man to have given up so much for his sake. I learned to my amazement that he was a boy of seventeen! The marriage had been arranged by a "go-between." He was the youngest of four brothers, who were all married; there were eleven adults and about twenty-five children all living in a little tiny cabin. The new wife had had to give her own little house to her father-in-law, who let it, and pocketed the rent, and she had not even a candle to work by in the winter evenings. I expressed surprise, but was looked at with astonishment. "But she was an old maid; and no Russian likes to be an old maid."

A peasant woman whom I knew wished to arrange a marriage for me! I am afraid I should have been rather a disturbing element in the cabin.

The maids in the nursery used always to tell me if any man paid them attentions, and just for all the world like an anxious mother, I used to make enquiries about his character, temper, position in life, and whether the would-be suitor could give his wife a home of her own.

If satisfied on these points I made no objection, but allowed the wooing to continue, but I would never hear of allowing any of them to go to live in the country with her husband's relations, and be treated as a beast of burden. One of the under-nurses was married last year. She had come to the palace straight from her school, at seventeen years of age, and was there for nearly seven years. She was naturally very much attached to the children, and when her last day came was in floods of tears all through the day, and the children were terribly distressed to see her in such grief. The little Grand Duchess Tatiana told her she could stay on if she liked, she knew we all loved her and would be sorry to part from her; and then she came running to me to beg me not to send dear Tegla away. I answered that she might stay if she liked, but that she had promised to marry Vladislav; it was her own wish, and I did not think she would like to break her word.

The other girls gave a little party to celebrate her leaving us, and the young man was amongst the guests. When the girl heard that he had arrived her grief broke forth again. She realised that the time of parting had come, and the children cried most bitterly. Little Tatiana Nicolaivna took a sheet of paper and a pencil, and wrote with great difficulty a letter which I translate: "Vladislav, - be good with Tegla -Tatiana." She placed this letter in an envelope and printed in large letters on the envelope, Vladislav, and sent it to him by the housemaid. I went in later to speak to the man and wish him happiness. He pulled this letter out of his pocket, and with tears in his eyes begged me to thank the little Grand Duchess, and assure her that he would never forget to be good to Tegla. All the more, because it was Tatiana Nicolaivna's wish. He always carries the letter about with him. She came to visit us several times after her marriage and was very happy. Whenever she writes she always sends a special message to Tatiana to say that Vladislav is very good to her, and the little one looks so pleased and says, "Well, I am glad."

The children used to make their own Christmas and birthday presents for their parents, generally some needlework. Once the little Grand Duchess Olga, in spite of my remonstrance, worked a kettle-holder for the Emperor. It had a little kettle singing on a fire, and "Polly, put the kettle on," worked on it, and she grounded it in blue. I made it up for her with a ruche of blue ribbon all round, and she admired it immensely.

When Christmas came she presented it to her father, saying, "Nana is afraid it won't be much use to you, it is a kettle-holder, but you can put it on your table for a mat, or hang it on the wall for a picture. Just see the pretty little frame round it."

One day the children and I were walking in the garden of the Winter Palace. The Emperor has some really beautiful collie dogs, and these were taking exercise in the garden at the same time. One of them, a young untrained creature, jumped on Tatiana Nicolaivna's back, and threw her down. The child was frightened and cried most bitterly. I lifted her up and said:

"Poor Sheilka! She did not mean to hurt you; she only wanted to say 'Good-morning' to you."

The child looked at me and said, "Was that all? I don't think she is very polite; she could have said it to my face, not to my back. "

Shortly after I first went to Russia the little Grand Duchess Olga was very naughty. I said to her, "I am afraid you got out of bed with the wrong foot foremost this morning." She looked a little puzzled, but said nothing. Next morning, before getting out of bed, she called me and asked which was her right foot.

I showed her, and she most carefully descended on it. "Now," said she, "that bad left foot won't be able to make me naughty to-day; I got out on the right."

It was only necessary to remind her of the fact all day to ensure perfect obedience.

I do not suppose that the world holds anyone more unmusical than I am. My singing might, without in any way violating the second commandment, be worshipped, for it is like nothing in the heavens above, nor in the earth beneath, nor in the waters under the earth. Gilbert might have had some dim prophetic sense of its beauty when he wrote:

"It was wild, it was fitful, as wild as the breeze; It wandered about into several keys; It was jerky and spasmodic, and harsh, I'm aware, Yet still it distinctly suggested an air."

I have just a faint idea of two tunes. One of them is "Rock of Ages"; the other, "Villikins and his Dinah."

The Grand Duchess Tatiana was ill one time and slept badly. I was up a good deal through the nights with her. She always asked me to sing for her, and I sang "Rock of Ages" till the poor little sufferer rebelled, and flatly refused to listen to it anymore, so I fell back upon "Villikins." It interested her very much, but she always asked, "Why did poor Dinah drink the poison cold?" I used to say to her, "She had not time to warm it, darling; now go to sleep."

One night, however, her enquiries went further, and "Why didn't she get her Nana to warm it for her? You would have warmed it for me, wouldn't you? "

I had got from England a preparation for the children's hair, and was rubbing it into little Anastasie's head one evening. She objected, and I said, "It will make your hair grow nicely, darling," so she submitted. Next evening I went to get the kappuka from the cupboard, and mademoiselle ran off into the next room. She returned dragging by its leg an awful dolly, a regular fetish, minus a wig, one eye, and an arm. She gravely took a little piece of sponge and began to rub the kappuka into the creature's head. I remonstrated, telling her I had to send to England for the stuff and did not want it wasted. She looked at me most reproachfully, and said, "My poor Vera! She has got no curls; this will make her hair grow." Of course, she got her way.

I have already spoken of the children's education, and I reproduce here a copy of a letter I had from the Grand Duchess Olga during my summer holidays, which is nicely written and expressed for a little girl of her age. Her Russian is further advanced than her English, as I had not much time to devote to her lessons. I also print some of her drawings.

Chapter XXX: Education in Russia

SECONDARY and the higher education are very well provided for in Russia. There are many universities, and the fees for tuition, books, etc., are low, only about twenty pounds per annum, nor is age any barrier to entrance. I think it would add to the usefulness of the universities if entrance were more difficult, for they get many students who must of necessity fail. There are very many free scholarships.

On one occasion I received a request from a young woman to get her name placed in the free list of a certain professor whom I happened to know. She was thirty years of age, and had left school at seventeen with very good certificates. She learned dressmaking, and was working in the country. She had saved some hundreds of roubles and wished to come to St. Petersburg to study medicine. I sent her word that for that a knowledge of Latin was necessary. She had already left school thirteen years, and had been living in the country where she had little access to books. She seemed to have been successful with the dressmaking, and why not stick to it? But she was ambitious, and would not be persuaded. She was perfectly certain she could learn all that would be required, and was determined to enter college.

I was very sorry for the girl coming up to St. Petersburg to live, probably in an underground cellar, and spend her little money all to no avail. However, she entered the university as a free pupil. Of course, she did no good, and took the place which might have been given to a younger pupil just left school, lost her dressmaking connection, tried the patience of her professors, and all to no purpose.

There are many educational institutions in St. Petersburg helped by the State; in these an excellent education is given, chiefly in modern and scientific lines. Foreign languages are well taught, and it is the exception to find an educated Russian who does not speak three or four languages fluently. Their own language is terribly difficult, and I never knew a Russian to whom figures were not a mighty stumbling-block. Even with their decimal system, which is so simple that we could master it in half an hour, they have to use in shops beads and wires for counting, and even with this help they go astray. When they come over to this country, how they get to understand our complicated money system I do not know.

There are many free scholarships in these schools. The Emperor and Empress have the right of presenting free pupils. On payment of a small sum by parents or relations a child can be received. One of the Russian nurses in the palace lately got a peasant child admitted into a school in this way. She was twelve years of age and could read, but not write. She was elected for eight years, was to be lodged, fed, educated and clothed, taught either housework or sewing, and fitted out for the world. On the completion of her eight years she might, should she so desire, enter the university, and all that was paid for her was about five pounds a year. At twelve years old she was a little unkempt peasant, with a handkerchief tied round her head, her feet covered with bark shoes, and wearing bandages instead of stockings. She had never even seen a train, and the most wonderful thing she ever saw in all her life was a statue of one of the Emperors in one of the streets of St. Petersburg. She did not know the meaning of a shop, had never heard of buying anything anywhere but in a fair.

In the higher institutes scholarships are given strictly according to the rank of the father of the pupil. Thus in one, no one under the rank of a major has a chance of getting a daughter or son received, and so on. In the highest of all, the daughters of generals and foreign princesses are received. The Queen of Italy and her sisters were educated here. In all these institutions the pupils and teachers wear uniforms. Some of them don the very ugliest, most unbecoming shade of blue one can imagine.

In Russia every man has military rank. The little Grand Duchess Olga's tutors were supposed to be generals, and were called "Your Excellency." They wore the uniform of generals, but had a little button in front of the cap, placed in a different position from that of the real live military generals.

Many decorations are given for various services entitling free education to a son or daughter.

Foreigners are not given military rank. They come to give lessons, even in the early morning, dressed in evening clothes. The tail-coat, etc., is taken as a sort of uniform.

In comparison with secondary schools, primary schools are very few. There are many in which the only means of education for the poor is the village priest. The poor man is supposed to instruct them, but life is not long enough for that, and he has many other duties to perform besides teaching his own barbarians. He has to farm his own little plot of ground, and to make bargains with the people, so much for a wedding, so much for a funeral, to baptise and confirm their children, to bury the dead, to solemnise marriages, etc. The poor man has really not time for more than he does.

The Russians value education most highly, and consider it an inestimable benefit. A peasant woman once asked me if I could read and write; I answered in the affirmative, but mentioned that I could not read Russian, but only my own language and French. She looked round my room and at my books, and asked me in an awed tone if I had read all those. I said I had. So she exclaimed, "Oh! What good parents you have had. I also had very good parents, who sent me to school every day for four years, and I can read almost any book, and even the newspapers, and write a letter quite easily."

The following story was told me by the Empress. One morning there arrived on the train from the Caucasus a little girl aged eleven. She went to a porter and asked to be sent to the Minister of Education. He made some demur; the child said, with perfect gravity, "I have come from the Caucasus, ten days' journey, to be put to school; you must please get me an izvochick and send me to his house. The child took herself so seriously that the porter took her in the same manner, and putting her into a street carriage, sent her off. Arriving at the minister's house she had great difficulty in persuading the servant to let her in. But she succeeded, and he promised to let his master know that a little girl from the Caucasus wanted to see him.

At the moment the minister was engaged with the Empress's secretary, but he said the child could be shown in. She stated her case, and the minister, in much difficulty and greatly amused over the whole business, assured the child that he had no vacancy. But the little one was not to be denied. "You are the Minister of Education," cried she. "I have come from the Caucasus to be put to school; you must put me somewhere." The minister was terribly puzzled as to what to do with her, and tried to explain things; but she would hear nothing. The secretary interposed, and offered to pay for this anxious little scholar till a free vacancy could be found for her. A note was accordingly written to the mistress of a school and the child was sent off under escort of a footman to be put to school. Her joy was unbounded. The secretary immediately went down to Peterhoff, and asked to see the Empress on pressing business. He told her about the child and her ardent desire to be educated. Inquiries were made, the truth of the child's story established, and the Empress gave her a vacancy in one of her own schools.

It seemed that her two eldest sisters had been received into a local school, but there was no room for this little one. She took the fact greatly to heart and fretted herself ill. The priest and doctor did their best to pacify her, but she would not be gainsaid. In despair they had taken a quarter ticket for her to St. Petersburg, thinking that if she could only realise that it was impossible she might be reconciled to the "Will of God." Accordingly she came, but "God helps those who help themselves" proved true in her case, though, indeed, we may see God's will in what happened. She is now under the Empress's protection, and unless I am much mistaken the world will hear of her some day. She will not be easily discouraged nor cast down.

The Emperor established many schools and founded many scholarships in honour of the birth of the Czarovitch, Alexis Nicolavitch. I do not think anyone could desire a better endowment than a school founded in his name.

Chapter XXXI: The Birth of an Heir

ON the 12th August, 1904, the little Grand Duke. Czarovitch was born. It happened to be my birthday, and when I went to see the newborn prince and congratulate the Empress she said to me, "You see what a nice birthday present I have given you."

He was baptised when he was twelve days old. I have described the baptismal ceremony for little Marie, and his was just slightly more ceremonious. His gilt carriage was drawn by eight horses instead of six, and he was dressed in blue and white instead of pink; also, the decoration which he received from the Emperor was of a higher order.

The little sisters were delighted with the new brother, and made many quaint and critical remarks about him. They were at the baptism dressed in Russian Court costume of blue satin, brocaded in silver and trimmed with silver braid and buttons, and they wore silver shoes. Their head-dresses were of blue velvet embroidered with pearls; they looked very sweet and quaint.

The child had for his godfathers the King of Denmark, the King of England, the Emperor of Germany, the Grand Duke Alexis, the Emperor's uncle, and many godmothers, including Princess Victoria of Wales. He received the name of Alexis; he was the third born Czarovitch in the Romanoff dynasty. Michael, the first Romanoff's eldest son, was called Alexis; Peter the Great's eldest son, born Czarovitch, received it also, and this one, of course, had to get it. The name means "Bringer of Peace." I hope it may prove true.

He is a very beautiful boy. In the middle of the baptismal ceremony, when he was being anointed for the first time, he raised his hand and extended his fingers as though pronouncing a blessing. Of course, everyone said that it was a very good omen, and that he would prove to be a father to his people. God grant it, but not for many years to come.

When we came out of church it was raining hard, which they said was a very good omen, but it was not so nice for my white satin dress.

The dress worn on this occasion by those present far exceeded in beauty and grandeur anything I had ever seen before.

It was the little girls' first great ceremony, and we can judge how delighted they were with it all.

Shortly after the birth of the Czarovitch I left Russia owing to private and personal reasons. I was very sorry and grieved to say goodbye to the dear children whom I love so well

70605099R00079

Made in the USA
Lexington, KY
13 November 2017